PRAISE FOR
SAVING *Grace*

"In this deeply felt, compassionate, and sensible book, Kirsten Powers makes a case for opening ourselves up to the transformative power of grace and of goodness. Rooted in history, theology, and the lived experience of our fragmented time, Powers's book is bracing, elevating, and essential."

—Jon Meacham, Pulitzer Prize-winning
author of *The Soul of America*

"Powers brings clarity and a fresh understanding to an idea that has been too often invoked to maintain the status quo. She shows grace to be a powerful force for inner and outer transformation, and an essential companion to anyone working for a more just, equitable, and compassionate world. *Saving Grace* is a light on the path during this dark time in American history."

—Don Lemon, host of CNN's *Don Lemon Tonight*
and author of *This Is the Fire*

"True to form, Kirsten Powers refuses to allow the culture wars to cost us our shared humanity. This book is a courageous call to truth and love existing side by side."

—Kate Bowler, author of *No Cure for Being Human*

"A tour de force . . . With the dogged curiosity of a top journalist, Powers strips the concept of grace of its typical churchy flourish and reveals bare-knuckled wisdom for our transforming world. Peppered with her typical wit and touch of whimsy, *Saving Grace* takes on tough questions rising from today's headlines and reveals a profound new relationship among power, justice, and peace."

—Lisa Sharon Harper, president of Freedom Road and author of *Fortune*

"It is not often that intelligence and spirituality are put together as well as Kirsten Powers does in this highly engaging road map for pursuing a life of grace. *Saving Grace* is the book the world needs right now."

—Richard Rohr, author of *The Universal Christ*

"With passionate urgency, Powers puts grace in the center of national discussions about bigotry, division, and revenge, insisting that there is a way beyond rage toward healing. *Saving Grace* offers practical wisdom and the realistic hope that America might yet be saved."

—Diana Butler Bass, author of *Grateful*

"A bravura book that is at once a highly personal spiritual journey, a deep meditation on grace, and a fascinating compendium of hard-won spiritual wisdom and practical advice . . . With her sparkling prose and heartfelt stories, Kirsten Powers shows us how the spiritual way is the most practical way to live."

—James Martin, SJ, author of *Learning to Pray*

SAVING
Grace

SAVING
Grace

Speak Your Truth, Stay Centered,
and Learn to Coexist
with People Who Drive You Nuts

KIRSTEN POWERS

CONVERGENT
New York

2023 Convergent Books Trade Paperback Edition

Copyright © 2021 by Kirsten Powers

All rights reserved.

Published in the United States by Convergent Books, an imprint of
Random House, a division of Penguin Random House LLC, New York.

CONVERGENT BOOKS is a registered trademark and its C colophon
is a trademark of Penguin Random House LLC.

Originally published in hardcover in the United States by Convergent Books, an
imprint of Random House, a division of Penguin Random House LLC, in 2021.

LIBRARY OF CONGRESS CATALOGING-IN-PUBLICATION DATA

Names: Powers, Kirsten, author.
Title: Saving grace / Kirsten Powers.
Description: First edition. | New York: Convergent, 2021 |
Includes bibliographical references.
Identifiers: LCCN 2021031950 (print) | LCCN 2021031951 (ebook) |
ISBN 9780593238233 (hardcover) | ISBN 9780593238240 (ebook)
Subjects: LCSH: Social conflict—United States—History—21st century. |
Polarization (Social sciences)—United States—History—21st century. |
United States—Social conditions—21st century. | Political culture—
United States—History—21st century. | Grace (Theology)
Classification: LCC HN90.P57 P69 2021 (print) |
LCC HN90.P57 (ebook) | DDC 303.60973—dc23
LC record available at https://lccn.loc.gov/2021031950
LC ebook record available at https://lccn.loc.gov/2021031951

Trade paperback ISBN 978-0-593-23825-7

Printed in the United States of America on acid-free paper

crownpublishing.com

1st Printing

Book design by Alexis Capitini

To Robert—for your endless grace

CONTENTS

AUTHOR'S NOTE

Striving to live a life oriented toward grace began for me purely as an act of self-preservation and survival following the 2016 election. I didn't have the capacity to continue engaging with what was happening in the world without feeling miserable and run-down. The judgmental soundtrack looping in my brain was stripping my life of joy. I often felt hopeless and helpless when I thought about the fate of our country.

I knew I had a real problem when I noticed I wasn't seeing people as complex human beings but rather as the sum total of their behavior or beliefs that enraged me. I fixated on what I believed about them and what I believed about myself. It usually went something like this: they are terrible/bad-intentioned/selfish people, and I am good/well intentioned/concerned about others. This automatic judgment led me to feel contempt and scorn and, at times, hatred.

Besides doing nothing to alleviate my misery—and as I would learn, was actually contributing to it—this mindset was at odds with my values. I needed a new framework through which to experience the world. I had an intuition that what I, and our culture at large, needed more of was *grace*.

I headed down this path reluctantly and haltingly and, at many points in the journey, considered turning back.

But ultimately, embracing grace as my lodestar ended up being a life-transforming experience, bringing emotional and physical healing to myself and relationships that I had almost written off as lost causes. The space in between self-preservation and transformation was filled with personal reckonings and revelations, emotional contractions and expansions, despair and elation.

Grace radically changed the way I see the world and what is possible for us.

What I offer here are not moral judgments, but practical insights and possible solutions. I draw on the wisdom tradition of Christianity, but I've done my best to make this book accessible to people of all faiths and to those with no faith at all. The context of the book is political and ideological disputes and division, but the tools I share could work for any kind of difficult situation or relationship.

I don't believe that my ideas are "right" and that people who do things differently are "wrong." As you will see, one of the first things I had to do on my journey toward grace was give up my reflexive dualistic thinking, which caused me to see the world through a starkly black-and-white lens. It was a world devoid of nuance.

When I wanted to learn about the power of grace in the face of grave wrongs and evil, I found myself drawn to civil rights icons like Rev. Dr. Martin Luther King Jr., the late Rep. John Lewis, and Ruby Sales. I was moved by the theology of Howard Thurman, one of Dr. King's mentors. I read books and sought out wisdom from all kinds of other people as well, but I raise the civil rights heroes specifically because I know how our culture has whitewashed their words to suit the ends of those in power.

I know that Dr. King is all too often selectively quoted to make him seem less radical than he was and to misrepresent what he believed. I know how the styles of Dr. King and Malcolm X are cast in stark binaries—one is good and the other is bad—and that is not my view.

When I draw on the wisdom of civil rights icons, it is because they hold a singular position in the history of this country. They have stared the Devil in the eyes and said, "Not today." Then they did it again. And again. And again. They never lost their humanity or became filled with bitterness while facing down cruelty, oppression, and dehumanization. Their spiritual worldview resonates with me and challenged me in a way that I needed to be challenged. Specifically, they gave me a different perspective on my reflexive need to demonize and *despise* people who were expressing views or engaging in behavior I found harmful. When these civil rights leaders talk about God, it is a God with whom I relate. They talk about a Jesus and a Christianity I recognize—one that hasn't been distorted and destroyed by the need to dominate and control.

They give me hope for myself, for you, and for our country.

There are, no doubt, ideas in this book that with the passing of time I may see differently. After all, I am not the same person I was even two years ago. She at least seems familiar to me. The me of ten years ago is a complete and utter stranger. I know I will continue to grow and change. I also know that even the best of intentions cannot lessen the negative impact that our words or actions may have. If I have expressed myself in a way that is hurtful or misinformed, please call me in or call me out—with a little grace, I hope.

Finally, I want to make clear that this book is not the last word on grace, but rather an opening volley. It chronicles a swimming-against-the-tide journey to attain a more grace-filled state in a culture that is being torn apart at the seams. It's the fruit of interviews with sociologists, theologians, activists, psychologists, trauma specialists, meditation teachers, peace and reconciliation experts, and religious leaders.

I've distilled my research, along with my own experiences, into what I hope will be a road map toward a little bit more grace. After all, if I could manage to figure out how to use grace to buffer the blows in the fight-club arena of American politics and media, then it just might be possible for you to do the same in your part of the world.

SAVING
Grace

Chapter 1

THE THICKNESS OF GRACE

We live in an atmosphere choked with the fumes of ungrace.
—PHILIP YANCEY[1]

G race is what makes human coexistence possible.
   Every thriving relationship in history—between friends, family, communities, and countries—has been saturated with grace. Grace is what lets us stumble, fall, get back up, and try again. Grace is what welcomes you back after you have failed someone or failed yourself.

Grace is what the Franciscan priest and writer Richard Rohr calls "the 'x' factor." It knits families, friendships, and countries back together after betrayal, hurt, and even violence. It's the father running to embrace the prodigal son when he's starving, penniless, and drenched in shame.[2] It's refusing to reduce people to the sum of their worst actions. We see it in the humility of the utterance "There but for the grace of God go I."

True grace is otherworldly. It goes against every instinct we have to seek revenge for wrongs or to shame and humiliate people who have acted immorally or unethically. It is what the theologian Dorothee Sölle, who grew up in Nazi Germany, called "borrow[ing] the eyes of God."[3] It enables us to see the divinity in every person, no matter what they've done, what they believe, or who they voted for. Grace is giving other people space to not be you.

Grace is the original self-care. It shushes the hectoring inner critic that tells us we are too much, too little, too fat, too thin, too good, and not good enough. Grace invites us off the hedonic treadmill of relentless achievement and success, which never delivers the happiness it promises. Grace doesn't care what size your waist is and celebrates every new wrinkle as evidence of wisdom earned. Grace shrugs at your unachieved New Years' resolutions and teaches you to be kind to yourself, just because. Grace reminds you of the "love yourself" part of Jesus's command "Love others as much as you love yourself."[4]

Grace is amazing.

It's the sweet sound that cracks open a hardened heart. It smooths the edges of rough regret about the things we did and the things we failed to do. It gives us permission to accept that we were doing the best we could with the information we had—or as Maya Angelou said, "You did . . . what you knew how to do, and when you knew better, you did better."[5] Grace tills the ground so that peace, wholeness, and completeness can take root in our burdened bodies, relationships, and the world.

Reduced to its absolute essence, grace is "unmerited favor." In the Christian tradition, it's what God gives us free of charge. But in a country that fetishizes accomplishment, tells people they can "hustle and grind" their way to worth, and fancies itself a meritocracy, many—like the prodigal son's older brother—are offended by the idea that other people would get something they haven't earned.

Practicing grace, in other words, can be really freaking hard.

It's something we love to receive, but often the last thing most of us want to offer. Instead, we incline ourselves toward what the author Philip Yancey calls "ungrace," withholding that which the world desperately needs. We become the prodigal's older brother glowering in the background, jealous and fuming about how undeserving his younger brother is of his father's reflexive affection and forgiveness. Ungrace has become the lingua franca of our discourse. More often than not, it's the lens through which we view people who don't share our religious, political, or moral values. Those people may be our leaders, co-workers, neighbors, or increasingly, members of our own families.

"Our lack and misunderstanding of grace and shrunken capacity to give grace is one of the things that makes the world such a brutal place," Lisa Sharon Harper, the writer and antiracism leader, told me in late 2020. "Discernment is necessary. Judgment is vanity."[6]

Yet our mortal daily bread is to sit in judgment of "bad" people, to call out those who hold "bad" beliefs, and to punish people who have done "bad" things. This is what the "good guys" do. Doing so makes us feel strong and righteous, like we are on the side of the angels.

Until it doesn't.

"WE WILL LEARN TO LIVE together, cooperate with one another, and recognize the dignity of others, or we will perish," wrote former president Barack Obama in his 2020 memoir, *A Promised Land*.[7]

The stakes for us really are that high, both personally and as a country.

It would be hard to overstate just how much some Americans have come to despise each other, at least in the abstract. In a January 2019 paper, "Lethal Mass Partisanship," researchers asked Republicans and Democrats if they believed that members of the opposing party were "just worse for politics" or "downright evil."[8] More than 40 percent in each party chose "downright evil." Twenty percent of Democrats and 15 percent of Republicans agreed with the statement

"We'd be better off as a country if large numbers of the oppos-ing party in the public today just died."

Online culture often reflects and feeds the hatred opposing political factions have for each other. But even within like-minded communities, purity spirals can lead to ostracizing, bul-lying, shaming, and deplatforming people. When it's at its best, social media is a revolutionary tool for much-needed account-ability, as we saw with #BlackLivesMatter and #MeToo. At its worst, it imitates the warped values of our inhumane criminal justice system and confuses cruel and disproportionate retribu-tion with accountability and justice. This behavior occurs across the political spectrum and in nonpolitical online com-munities.

In hindsight, it's perversely fitting that the King of Internet Trolls became president of the United States. We were already teetering on the edge, but our public discourse indisputably took a turn for the worse when Donald Trump took up resi-dence at 1600 Pennsylvania Avenue. The political became ex-trapersonal as many people started to experience serious fractures in their relationships with family, friends, co-workers, and neighbors.

All around Washington, DC, where I live, yard signs reading HATE HAS NO HOME HERE began to crop up in 2017. Donald Trump's name didn't appear anywhere in the design, but the message was an obvious reference to the president and his fol-lowers. A longtime friend, a moderate Democrat who is one of the most even-tempered people I know, joked to me that at his lowest point he felt like posting a sign that read, "Hate *has* a home here," giving voice to a shared rage about what Donald Trump had wrought in this country.

My friend was worn out, and so was I. Whereas I used to go on air to discuss things like health care or foreign policy, with the election of Trump, I now spent the bulk of my time having to react to the president's latest tweet or push back against the shameless lying from an endless succession of Trump apologists. I was emotionally exhausted, frustrated, and angry a lot of the time, like so many others around me. I was hearing more and more, "I can't live like this anymore." The fractures were compounding, and people were finding themselves estranged from others who were important to them. If this agitation, fear, and rage had been helping anyone or any causes I cared about, perhaps it would have seemed worth it. But it wasn't.

"Let no man pull you so low as to hate him," Booker T. Washington once warned.[9] Well, I went that low. And then some. On good days, I could limit my negative feelings about those who I felt were causing so much harm to mere disdain. On the worst days, I hated their guts. But feeling hate, like being unforgiving, is tantamount to drinking poison and waiting for the other person to die. It only deepened my misery.

Reluctantly, I had a dawning awareness of just how devoid of grace our culture was. My initial attitude was "Save grace for the saints." My temperament is much more Joan of Arc than Jesus. I'm more inclined to saddle up and go to war to protect my people than to turn the other cheek or love my enemies.

While grace was a difficult proposition even before Trump moved into the White House, the notion has seemed that much more far-fetched since he engulfed the public consciousness and dominated our public discourse. While some hoped that his dethroning would bring a reprieve, his refusal to admit defeat drove the wedge deeper. Talking about grace in this kind of environment can almost feel wrongheaded, like throwing down one's sword in the midst of battle.

But it's actually the opposite. Now is exactly the time we need to be laboring to create more grace in our lives and culture at large.

What makes finding grace for others feel so impossible is that we are usually called upon to offer it when confronted with someone who has deeply threatened our sense of right and wrong. Grace exists especially for the person who we may feel is uniquely unworthy of it, who has done or said something repulsive or harmful to us, and who in some cases we're still bound to dislike. But because it is unmerited favor, if we can come up with a reason why a person deserves grace, then it's probably not grace.

What I came to realize is that many of us have a lot of confusion and misconceptions about what the word *grace* actually means. Just as important as describing what grace *is* is naming what grace is *not*.

Grace is not something you do just to benefit other people. It's good for *you*. It's a liberating inner orientation.

Grace helps you see that other people's beliefs and actions belong to them, and that marinating in judgment, rage, hatred, frustration, and resentment toward them helps nobody. In fact, it harms you. If you are anything like me, it steals your peace, makes your body hurt, creates a sense of helplessness and hopelessness, causes anxiety, and in the worst-case scenario leads you to adopt the behavior and tactics you are trying to oppose. Philosopher Friedrich Nietzsche warned that if you are going to fight the monster, you need to make sure that in the process you don't become the monster. Grace creates a buffer zone between you and the people who are driving you to the edge and even causing serious harm. Practicing grace protects your energy, so you can put it toward something more beneficial than furiously typing mean tweets, raging at a family member with a problematic or offensive worldview, or screaming at the television every night.

Grace is not just about external behavior.

I've had people praise me for my grace in contentious on-air interactions where I was, in fact, seething with hatred and contempt. Operating from a position of grace may help you be more courteous or calm in the face of difficult situations, but if your internal monologue is about how evil or horrible other people are, then you aren't really experiencing them through the lens of grace.

Grace is first and foremost a matter of the heart. It's an orientation toward the world and other people. When Jesus said to love your enemies, he wasn't talking about the love we have for friends or family or chocolate. He was talking about what the Greeks called *agape,* or as Martin Luther King Jr. described it, "redeeming good will for all [people]."[10] *Agape* is seeing the divine spark in other people, no matter how you feel about them. "Loving is not liking," as Richard Rohr likes to say. So it is with grace. And yes, it can often be as hard as it sounds.

That said, grace does not mean you have to check your passionate beliefs or personality at the door. You still get to have big emotions and strong opinions and throw a serious side-eye when it's needed. You don't have to ditch your dry sarcasm or devastating wit. You aren't required to be pious or earnest. You can still be irreverent and flawed and messy. Grace creates space for all of us. Yes, I *will* still be making horrified faces when another guest says something batshit crazy while I'm on CNN. Yes, I *will* sometimes still curse under my breath as I exit the set.

Grace does not ask you to accept the status quo.

It doesn't mean choosing neutrality in the name of peace. It doesn't "tone-police" people when they express outrage over injustice, abuse, or harm—demanding that their complaints be expressed only in a way that doesn't make anyone uncomfortable. It doesn't encourage dispassion or silence in the face of wrongdoing. Being filled with anger when encountering injustice is normal—and, I will argue, healthy and good. All the more so today. The old activist dictum "If you aren't pissed off, you aren't paying attention" is a sentiment that resonates strongly with me. It's when that righteous anger starts tilting into self-righteousness, judgment, and hatred that we are in the danger zone, both personally and as a country.

The word *judgment* can cause some confusion, so let me clarify. When I identify it as a problem, I am talking about being judgmental, not making a clear-headed judgment. The latter looks like discernment, which is having clarity about a situation or person; the former requires you to put yourself above another to look down on them. Being judgmental comes with an emotional charge such as annoyance, disgust, or even revulsion. Discernment, on the other hand, is calm, dispassionate, and clear. It provides information.

Grace is also not a "get out of jail free" card; it's not the word you wave in the face of someone who has been harmed in an effort to shut them down. In fact, if you are ever demanding grace from another person, you've missed the whole point. We all need to be focused on how *we* can pour more grace into the world, not how we can wring it out of other people.

Cosmic grace—the kind dispensed by an all-loving God—costs nothing, but here on earth more is required to make amends when you have caused harm. Yes, grace creates the space for reconciliation, but not without repentance and repair from the person who inflicted the damage. We need to develop a culture that models this kind of accountability and provides a path to redemption for those willing to undertake the arduous process of making things whole where they have caused brokenness.

Grace offered reflexively without need for repentance or accountability is for minor offenses, such as lashing out at your spouse when you are in a bad mood. A simple apology will do, or if we are lucky our spouse will just ignore us. That kind of grace is essentially the grease of existence. We are all offering and receiving it on a near-daily basis. We might also see this kind of grace with a one-time offense that is more serious, where the person seems sincerely sorry. But once we move into the realm of repeated problematic or harmful behavior, grace looks like accountability. Grace-infused accountability, however, is different from the vengeful, overly punitive version we often see in our culture.

Too many of us have seen grace weaponized in efforts to avoid accountability. It has been invoked as a way of shaming and silencing people who express justified anger and make calls for accountability. When people from marginalized groups seek accountability for having been harmed by the words or behavior of others, they are too often admonished to show more "grace"—even though they have been bottomless reservoirs of the stuff since the beginning of time. Remember: grace is something you should be focused on giving, rather than obsessing about how others aren't offering it to you or those you like. I see this a lot on social media where people who regularly engage in nasty takedowns suddenly start preaching "grace and forgiveness" when someone is held accountable for engaging in racist or other bigoted behavior. This is an abuse of the idea of grace.

Grace does not create a false unity.

Following his election as president of the United States, Joe Biden began calling for unity among Americans. This call was not greeted enthusiastically by everyone. When people hear "unity," they reflexively imagine a kumbaya moment, where we all hold hands and sing, realizing that we really aren't that different after all.

Except, we really *are* that different, and most people have figured this out by now. We disagree about important issues, and there is no reason to pretend otherwise. Too often, *grace* is a word that gets thrown around when people in power want you to ignore the fact that someone did something terrible—like, say, incite a mob to storm the United States Capitol in an effort to overthrow an election and assassinate lawmakers.

President Biden attempted to clarify what he meant by "unity," telling reporters that it was important to try to "eliminate the vitriol" and "stay away from the ad hominem attacks on one another."[11] These are laudable goals, though I see taking these steps more as acts of grace than of unity. The dictionary definition of *unity* is "the state of being joined together or in agreement."[12] Does this sound remotely possible right now?

White House press secretary Jen Psaki's explanation was

probably closer to what many people understand the term to mean in the political context. "Unity is about the country feeling that they're in it together," she said. "I think we'll know that when we see it."[13]

But many people don't feel that it's possible to be "in it together" with large factions of their fellow Americans. I'm not "in it" with people who claim the election was stolen and who support voter suppression laws. I am not "in it" with white supremacists. I'm not "in it" with people who demonize undocumented immigrants as "invaders" or defend separating children from their parents when they cross the border.

Unity in such a situation is a metaphysical impossibility. We may all love America and want to see her flourish, but our visions of what that would look like are not just different, but in direct opposition. Our disagreements do not concern minor issues; they are about fundamental values.

The word *unity* can be particularly triggering to people who have been mistreated throughout history. Too often, the quest for unity has been used to justify ignoring the needs, dignity, and rights of certain groups of people. Bridge building is important work for those who feel called to it. The problem occurs when finding a middle ground means sacrificing the rights and dignity of marginalized groups of people.

As the bestselling author and antiracism leader Austin Channing Brown has written, "[Being a] bridge builder sounds appealing until it becomes clear how often that bridge is your broken back."[14] While many today pine for the "good old days" when there was less political rancor, much of that comity came at the expense of members of underrepresented communities.

As recently as the 1980s and '90s, Democrats and Republicans found unity in their belief that same-sex couples had no right to marry. The two parties were unified in their belief that it was fine for Congress, indeed the entire government, to be run almost completely by white men. They came together to demonize Black communities in the name of "law and order." Going back further, to the 1950s, which many conservatives hold up as the halcyon days of America, women were denied the most basic of rights and legal racial segregation reigned throughout the South.

Which is why I prefer the paradigm of grace to that of unity.

Practicing grace will never mean demanding that disenfranchised people seek unity, or even relationship, with people who would deny them their basic dignity and rights. Grace asks no one to find common cause with people who prioritize unity in the dominant culture over equality, justice, and the dignity of all human beings.

But even if we get clear on what grace is and what it's not, there are few practical road maps to show us how to generate and integrate grace in our lives.

When I decided to make grace my touchstone, I unknowingly fell back on flawed Christian teaching that has left many of us throwing up our hands and declaring grace an unachievable and impractical goal. I imagined that by engaging in Olympian amounts of prayer, meditation, church attendance, and consumption of spiritual texts I would be so filled up with the love of God, I'd just overflow with the stuff. I'd be a veritable human Pez dispenser of grace. The contempt coursing through my veins would drain out of me, and I'd be a new person.

I'll cut to the chase: it didn't work.

After a period of minimal change and maximum frustration, I realized I had in effect mapped out a plan to engage in spiritual bypassing, which is the "tendency to use spiritual ideas and practices to sidestep or avoid facing unresolved emotional issues, psychological wounds, and unfinished developmental tasks."[15] In the secular world, this phenomenon is sometimes referred to as "toxic positivity," which is "the excessive and ineffective overgeneralization of a happy, optimistic state across all situations [which results in] the denial, minimization, and invalidation of the authentic human emotional experience."[16] It's looking for the quick or magical fix so we don't have to do any deeper examination of ourselves or systemic problems in our culture.

Upon reflection, I realized I'd never seen spiritual practices alone transform a person into a paragon of grace. Some people I knew who we might describe as having grace just hated conflict or didn't care enough about even the most incendiary issues of the moment to develop an opinion, let alone self-righteously condemn or demonize someone who had an opposing view. Then there were the rare birds I knew who seemed to embody grace: a British atheist Zen Buddhist in New Mexico, a Coptic Christian in Egypt, and an Iranian American Muslim in Washington, DC. How did they come to be so grace filled?

I noticed they had a few things in common: They were spiritually grounded and humble. They had done the work of self-examination, getting real with themselves about their limitations, and doing the work to address them. They were openhearted and didn't engage in the kind of dualistic—"good vs. evil"—sorting that so many of us do, despite caring deeply about the level of suffering in the world. They didn't "other" people who held values with which they disagreed, and no matter how disturbed they might be by what was happening around them, they didn't become bundles of rage, anxiety, and hopelessness.

"You can't solve a problem with the same consciousness that created it" is a quote often attributed to Albert Einstein. What he seems to have actually said, in regard to the development of atomic weapons is "We shall require a substantially new manner of thinking if [humanity] is to survive."[17] Both formulations capture the essential task before us: in order to practice grace, we need a new way to think about the world, each other, and the challenges we face.

This book, then, is about unlearning many of our ingrained

ways of being, those that fuel the toxic levels of ungrace in our culture. It's about understanding how to stay grounded in the midst of the tornado; speak your truth without spitting contempt; and coexist with people you don't even want to share a planet with, let alone a country. *Coexist* means different things to different people—for me, and this book, it denotes living in peace with people you'd very much like to vote off the island. It's a society that rejects physical, psychological, emotional, cultural, and verbal violence.

The late civil rights icon and congressman John Lewis offered illumination of this pathway when he wrote in 2012: "Choose confrontation wisely, but when it is your time don't be afraid to stand up, speak up, and speak out against injustice. And if you follow your truth down the road to peace and the affirmation of love, if you shine like a beacon for all to see, then the poetry of all the great dreamers and philosophers is yours to manifest in a nation, a world community, and a Beloved Community that is finally at peace with itself."[18] Such a vision of our future can seem fantastical in the current environment, until we remember that John Lewis's wisdom was forged in the fiery struggle for freedom and equality in the Jim Crow South.

The extreme level of division in this country is causing misery for many of us and dysfunction in our government. But the goal of grace is not to erase differences. Rather, grace helps us navigate those differences while honoring the humanity of others and ourselves.

"Grace is to live in the possibility of what does not exist," Yale theologian Dr. Willie James Jennings told me in an interview. "Grace means that you can actually look at the other person recognizing that there's not only things that you don't like—but there's things that you hate—and still ask yourself: can I be open to the possibility that something can be created where there's nothing right now?"[19]

Even trying to see this possibility can seem like a bridge too far. We feel like a nation on life support, gasping for hope. In the near term, we just need to take it a day at a time. For some people, moving from hatred to neutrality would be a victory when it comes to how they feel about ideological or political foes.

But I think most of us realize on some level that we are made for more than the way we are living right now. The vision that Congressman Lewis cast causes a deep stirring in us because we long for a more transcendent existence that recognizes we are all interconnected, woven together by our humanity, whether we like each other or not. A life of purpose is one that seeks to create a Beloved Community—a just and equal society based on the love of one's fellow human beings, as articulated by Rev. Dr. Martin Luther King Jr.

I think we can—and in fact yearn to—go in a different direction than our narrow impulses often take us. We are ultimately meant to enter into what Dr. Jennings calls "the thickness of grace."

Chapter 2

A NATION DIVIDED
THAT WE CANNOT STAND

Something is rotten in the State of Denmark.

—The guard Marcellus in *Hamlet*[1]

Sometimes I really don't like people.

It doesn't help that often I see them at their worst, living as I do at ground zero of the political cage fight. Each day I grab an outfit from the rows of gumdrop-colored attire arrayed in my closet (the colors "pop" on television, so they say), suit up, and step into the ring in front of millions of people to analyze and debate the most contentious issues facing our country and world. On a good day, there will be civil disagreement. On a bad day, it's all-out trench warfare.

Like so many Americans, I found my bad days became far more common after the 2016 election.

For the last decade and a half, I have been a political analyst and columnist. After working in the Democratic political world for years—first as an appointee in the Clinton administration and later as a press aide on various New York City and state campaigns—I found myself at Fox News as a political analyst debating everything from Obamacare to immigration to tax policy to whether *Duck Dynasty* star Phil Robertson should lose his job for making homophobic comments.

On a typical segment, I faced down a minimum of one panelist who disagreed vehemently with my worldview, paired with a host who also happened to be sympathetic to the opposing view. On some shows the odds were even worse, with as many as four other panelists clamoring to disagree with whatever I said.

Usually nothing terribly interesting happened. But sometimes the conversation would go off the rails, including during my first ever guest-hosting gig filling in for the "left," represented by Alan Colmes, on the prime-time show *Hannity & Colmes*. When I repeatedly pressed Ann Coulter on how bad the Bush-era Afghanistan war was going, she ripped off her microphone and walked off during a live TV segment. In the break after the segment, as sweat pooled on my lower back, Sean Hannity kept shaking his head and murmuring, "You shouldn't have done that. You really shouldn't have done that." I assumed my nascent gig as a left-of-center voice at Fox was over. The opposite turned out to be true. The incident caught the eye of CEO Roger Ailes, and in late 2007 I signed on as a full-time political analyst at Fox News.

It was there that I had throwdowns with Bill O'Reilly on immigration, the drone war, and pretty much anything else that two people could argue about. One night, during a particularly explosive argument, O'Reilly claimed racism didn't exist in America, and I demanded he tell me how many Black friends he had, feeling sure that he had not had this view affirmed by anyone who wasn't white. (Spoiler alert: this enraged him.)

The absolute worst professional experience of my life was a feud on live television with Fox News host Megyn Kelly over whether the "New Black Panthers" were disrupting our electoral system. The video, which included Kelly threatening to cut my microphone after I criticized her for pushing the "scary Black man" trope, immediately went viral. As I stumbled off the set, clearly shaken by what had just occurred, I was met with clapping in the DC bureau's newsroom, a minor balm for what I had just experienced.

The *Washington Post*[2] described my approach at Fox News as "bright-eyed, sharp-tongued, [and] gamely combative" and called me "a ferocious advocate for her points of view."[3] In a 2015 profile, the *Post* offered a brisk biographical sketch: how I grew up in Fairbanks, Alaska, as the eldest child of two of the few liberals in town (they were archaeologists and professors of anthropology at the University of Alaska); how I found my way into working in Democratic politics, and from there to a career in on-air political commentary; how I'd traded in my atheism for Christianity a decade before. The piece also captured my mostly stoic outward demeanor accurately enough. I was cast as an iconoclast charting my own course, even if it was lonely. This certainly was the image I projected, because that's what I believed about myself at the time.

But that description ignored the inner turmoil I often experienced during segments on Fox. While I usually appeared placid and unflappable, my insides were often tied in knots of frustration. Worse, when you have disputes on cable television, the argument doesn't end when you walk off set. That's just the appetizer. What typically follows is a poisonous buffet of harassment on social media and via email. The appearances also generate praise, but typically it's hard to hear over the roar of fury coming your way.

A young journalism graduate student with a similar name, Kristen Powers, wrote about the emotional impact of online harassment when tweets meant for me ended up in her feed. Writing in *Bustle* in September 2016, she shared screenshots of tweets informing me I was a "loser" and "nuts" and how I was "dumb, blonde and liberal."[4] Those were the nicer ones. Kristen had understandably been unnerved by other, more threatening tweets such as "You are nothing but trash that needs to be discarded do yourself a favor suck on a bullet" and "I'd love to f—the liberal out of you."

When Kristen reached out to interview me for her story, we ended up grabbing drinks, and I assured her I just ignored the attacks since they didn't really affect me. I truly believed that at the time. It would take years for me to appreciate the serious emotional and physical toll that constant misogynist harassment was taking on me.

Balancing out the unpleasantness of much of what I dealt with on the prime-time shows was the work I did in the news division. I was a regular panelist on *Special Report with Bret Baier* and *Fox News Sunday with Chris Wallace,* shows I half-jokingly referred to as my "safe spaces" because disagreements were civil and I was given ample time to say my piece without obnoxious interruptions. I also regularly participated in special coverage of news events, including election night coverage of primaries and the general election, in which the theatrical antics of the prime-time entertainment shows were refreshingly absent. On the news shows, I worked with thoughtful conservatives such as Charles Krauthammer, George Will, and *The Weekly Standard*'s Steve Hayes and Bill Kristol. While we disagreed on most things, their arguments were reasoned and seldom over the top. Amiable chatting was the norm, on and off set, and I considered them friends.

One evening in early 2015, after a particularly bruising argument with O'Reilly, a friend texted me to say how increasingly disturbing he was finding my weekly segments on *The O'Reilly Factor.* He said something along the lines of "I really wish you wouldn't work there anymore. This is unhealthy." From where I'm sitting now, his concern makes perfect sense. But at the time I felt he was overreacting, especially since so many people—including *O'Reilly Factor* watchers—routinely deemed me the victor in these duels, as if that really mattered in the end. In reality, I was underreacting to the toxic elements of my work environment and misidentifying my attitude as grace. Looking back, I can see how confused I was about what grace actually entails.

An already stressful environment took a turn for the worse in the summer of 2015 when the reality TV star Donald Trump announced he was running for president and quickly started rising in the polls. I had no idea how much this turn of events would affect me and the country. Soon, Fox was in disarray as it came under attack by Trump for its less than worshipful coverage. (It's easy to forget that Fox was once anti-Trump.)

For the first time since I had joined the network, I started to feel a not-so-subtle pressure to pull my punches as executives tried to manage the Frankenstein's monster they had created by providing Trump a platform over the years on which he thrilled the right with his noxious "birther" conspiracy theory and other unhinged political commentary. My more thoughtful colleagues began to be replaced by reactionary Trump supporters who it seemed would say anything to please Trump and his supporters. My former "safe spaces" were now overrun with loudmouth radio hosts and other shameless Trump promoters.

One morning in 2016 after doing primary night election coverage, I awoke in a New York City hotel room and felt a hole where one of my teeth used to be. By the time I got to my dentist the next day, I was informed that I had been clenching my jaw so tightly that I broke a molar.

Even before Trump, I had decided I wanted to leave Fox, but I now realized the situation was completely untenable. I did what I should have done a long time ago: I began negotiations to get out of my contract, and while it took a little time, I finally was able to leave.

I was thrilled to immediately land at CNN, but I still had not outrun this relatively new breed of commentator: the professional Donald Trump defender. Almost exclusively men, they seemingly could not let a woman's sentence go uninterrupted.

These encounters made my typical pre-2016 days at Fox News look like *The PBS NewsHour*.

I began to notice a somewhat unfamiliar emotion—unalloyed rage—rising in me. Sometimes I would feel what I can only describe as hatred when I witnessed these commentators' shameless mendacity in defense of their man. I am not saying every person who appeared on CNN and defended Trump created this fury in me. I'm referring to a very specific type of person who seemed to come out of nowhere and didn't even pretend to care about facts.

They were driving me nuts.

I wasn't the only one. People of all political and ideological persuasions would email me or tweet at me following an appearance, expressing their outrage and frustration about the direction the Republican party was taking. Who were these people? Why were they saying these things that were so obviously untrue? How come people couldn't see how dangerously unfit Donald Trump was to lead the country?

What was happening?

Gone were the days of friendly chitchat with my ideological foes in the greenroom. When it came to the Trump defenders, I could barely mumble a "hello." I took no interest in their lives, asked them no questions about their families, and did my best to minimize my interaction with them.

My contempt had no partisan roots. I'd long been able to amicably debate and interact with Republicans. Perhaps more importantly, Donald Trump had no real partisan beliefs with which to disagree. The only thing he appeared to believe in was himself—even his defenders seemed to acknowledge this. Postappearance, they would often make a cleanup attempt as we took the elevator to the lobby. More than once, they'd sheepishly try to explain that they made their outlandish claims or denied reality because Trump had zero tolerance for disagreement or criticism.

This just left me feeling further enraged.

Among Republicans I knew, there was real panic and confusion. I watched while their longtime friendships frayed and even unraveled as people sorted themselves into Never Trumpers, Trump collaborators, and full-blown Trump supporters. Democrats looked on with more than a little bit of schadenfreude, believing the seeming implosion of the Republican party would redound to their benefit when Hillary Clinton mopped the floor with the clownish candidate GOP voters had sent into the ring.

It became abundantly clear just how much the political ground had shifted a month before Election Day 2016. I was sitting on a CNN set, waiting to discuss some routine topic, when the host suddenly announced we had breaking news. Stupefied, I watched as tape rolled showing Donald Trump making vulgar comments about a woman reporter who was about to interview him for *Access Hollywood*. Was I really going to have to offer commentary about a presidential candidate who had in the past gleefully described grabbing women by the p—sy?

Yes, I was.

I served up a withering analysis of the behavior on that tape. From that day forward, I was on the receiving end of an almost nonstop online assault from Trump's army of supporters. It got worse in early January 2017, when the president-elect unleashed his full fury on CNN, characterizing it as "fake news" and a "terrible" organization during a press conference.[5] A month later as president, he named CNN an "enemy of the American people" along with the three broadcast networks and the *New York Times*.[6]

America felt as divided and toxic as it had ever been in my lifetime. Little did I know, we were just getting warmed up.

Donald Trump started his presidency with what would come to be known as his "American Carnage" inaugural speech— a dark, divisive rant that former president George W. Bush reportedly called "some weird shit." Life post-2016 often felt like a perpetual *Alice in Wonderland* experience, where up was down and black was white. Every day brought a new norm-shattering comment or action by the president, reliably accompanied by hypocritical and jaw-dropping defenses from Republicans who seemed content to be dragged low by their new standard-bearer.

While America was hardly a Valhalla of comity before Trump, there is no question he quickly became a dividing line in many relationships. Sixteen percent of Americans told pollsters they had stopped talking to a family member or friend because of the 2016 election.[7] A private Facebook group, Wives of the Deplorables, cropped up in 2019 to provide a space for women married to Trump-supporting men to commiserate and seek support in navigating political disagreements that had overtaken their previously happy marriages.[8]

On dating apps, profiles took on an unusually political flavor. Shortly after Trump moved into the White House, the dating site OkCupid reported a 64 percent increase in dating profiles featuring political terms.[9] "Swipe left if you voted for Donald Trump,"[10] started cropping up in online dating bios, and new dating platforms emerged that tailored to specific groups, such as Donald Dater and TrumpSingles.[11]

Looking back, I knew we weren't in Kansas anymore the day I ordered someone to leave my house after I found out he voted for Donald Trump.

For the previous six years, Mark had solved pretty much any problem I faced relating to my home. While he hung curtains or assembled furniture or painted a wall, we would talk about faith, books, movies—and, being in DC, politics. Mark was a Republican, so we tended not to see things the same way, but that never posed a problem. His day job was as a book publicist—he moonlighted as a handyman—and I was always interested to hear about his authors, many of whom came from the world of politics.

Then, one October evening in 2018, Mark was fixing the garbage disposal and we began chatting about the day's news. I said something critical about Trump, figuring that we would agree, since nearly all my criticisms of Trump had nothing to do with core Republican policy but instead were about his temperament, bigotry, demagoguery, and nonstop lying.

I had no reason to expect that Mark would be different from the vast majority of my DC–based Republican friends, who had been charter members of the Never Trump movement. It was strange to no longer be at odds with them politically, since in many ways their ire for Trump ran the deepest of all: he was not only destroying the country they loved but also making a mockery of their political party and their Christian faith.

After I made my remark about Trump, Mark started pushing back. While he was saying words that turned into sentences, none of it made sense to me. The more I listened, the more I felt like I had heard this before. Then it hit me: he sounded like the Trump Republicans I went up against on television.

I must be imagining this, I thought.

But he kept talking, and the blood began rushing to my head. "Did you vote for Trump?" I finally half-whispered. Mark nodded in silent assent. "How could you?" I asked, my voice rising. "I thought you were a Christian!"

Then the words escaped my mouth: "I need you to leave my house." I was taken aback by the strength of my reaction. I hurried up the stairs to my bedroom in an effort to end the confrontation. I felt shaky as I heard Mark slowly packing up his things. I sat on my bed, stunned. What was happening? I had never ordered someone out of my home before. I went back downstairs and apologized for my outburst. Mark was gracious and said he could explain to me why he felt the way he did. I wasn't interested.

I had zero bandwidth for this. While Trump had been president for only a little over a year and a half, it had already felt like ten lifetimes. Though I thought I'd grown accustomed to nasty online attacks, the degree of misogyny and rage coming at me from Trump supporters was next level, even for Twitter. Six months into the Trump administration, I had sat in my living room in a numb kind of horror as DC police officers explained in detail how I needed to upgrade my security system. They were concerned because a white supremacist "alt-right" online community with a history of violence had posted my address and my phone number online, along with pictures of my home and my dog, suggesting that people pay me a visit. These kinds of experiences were becoming routine for many journalists. The situation had gotten worse over the last year.

Mark hadn't been aware of any of this. He made some attempt to explain his support for Trump, and I cut him off again. The solution to our disagreement, I said, was simple: we would never talk about Donald Trump again.

It was an edict. It wasn't up for debate.

The constant gaslighting of the Trump era was taking a toll on me, and I wasn't about to listen to it in my home. The neverending fusillade of lies, increasingly hard even to keep track of, was beginning to feel like a tactical maneuver intended to wear down truth itself. I was at my wit's end listening to the president of the United States make racist claims that a caravan of desperate refugees was going to "invade" the country. For that matter, I was still recovering from the previous month of covering the contentious hearings to confirm Brett Kavanaugh to the Supreme Court.

Like so many, I had been deeply disturbed by how Republicans handled the hearings because of the message being sent to the world—in particular teenage boys—about how callously sexual assault allegations would be treated by certain national leaders. I was sexually assaulted in high school and had never spoken of it to anyone. As I watched Christine Blasey Ford maligned by Kavanaugh supporters, I decided it was time to speak out about what had happened to me.

I recounted in my *USA Today* column how I, like Ford, could recall little more from my sexual assault than who did it and what they did.[12] I couldn't tell you in whose house or in what

neighborhood it happened. I don't know what month it occurred, and I could only guess at the year. I didn't report the
assault to the police or to anyone else. All of this is typical of
women who have been sexually assaulted, yet Kavanaugh supporters would not relent in their campaign to cast Ford as some
troubled ditz who couldn't get her facts straight. Indeed, the
day after my column ran, the president of the United States
mimicked Ford at a rally, playing her account of being sexually
assaulted for laughs and applause.[13]

I was at whatever the place is after you reach the end of your
rope when my then-CNN colleague Rick Santorum told me in
the greenroom, between segments, that Ford was likely making
these allegations because she believed she would become a
feminist hero and get rich on the speaking circuit and selling
books.

"Because accusing powerful men of sexual assault is the path
to success," I sarcastically retorted. I was furious. This was an
old sexist canard that ignored the reality that most women are so
painfully aware of the consequences of speaking up about harassment or assault that, until recently, they usually stayed silent.[14]

Around this time, a Catholic theologian I infrequently corre-
sponded with texted me his belief that it was obvious the
"boys" had just been horsing around, probably playing a game,
with Ford. "What 'game' involves pushing a teenage girl into a
bedroom, pinning her down on a bed, groping her, and covering her mouth so she can't scream?" I typed into my phone.
"What 'game' is it where when she tries to escape multiple
times she is thwarted?" He wasn't even bothering to claim it
didn't happen. He was arguing that her allegations, even if true,
were insignificant. It wasn't like he was from another era. He
was in his early forties.

I was in a near-constant state of agitation, emotionally exhausted and overwhelmed with contempt. If someone had
suggested at that point that I needed to incorporate grace into
my life, I would have thought they'd lost their damn minds.

Chapter 3

BEYOND GOOD AND EVIL

Dualistic thinking works well for the sake of simplification
and conversation, but not for the sake of truth or the immense
subtlety of actual personal experience.

—RICHARD ROHR[1]

*T*here are two kinds of people in the world, as the joke goes: people who think there are two kinds of people, and people who don't.

We love to sort people and ideas into opposing baskets. Dualistic thinking rules our discourse in a way that makes it almost impossible to have a discussion about controversial topics—and let's face it: these days, almost any topic can invite controversy.

Even, as it turns out, the topic of grace.

When I began to publicly express the need for more grace in our culture in early 2019, I repeatedly heard some version of the idea that I was telling people to "go hug a Nazi." "Oh, so if people were just nicer to Hitler, everything would have been different" was a typical sentiment. I get it. This was the same reflexive resistance I'd initially experienced as it slowly dawned on me that grace could be the antidote to not just my own misery but also the struggles of our current age.

Some of this reaction may have been a result of the baggage the word *grace* can carry—including the misconception that it's a synonym for *nice*—but our tendency to resort to binary extremes likely played a role too. It's why if someone had mentioned the word *grace* to me in the fall of 2018, I would have been repelled and maybe even offended. I would have assumed they didn't grasp the seriousness of the issues the country faced. I could see only two opposing choices: domination and demonization or apathy and acquiescence.

I—like so many people—*just was not in the mood for grace*.

But the reality is, integrating grace into our lives and our broader culture provides a world of options that don't include abandoning all our principles or becoming doormats. However, the all-or-nothing paradigm is the default for many Americans, and it becomes even more so under duress. You either completely embrace and excuse other people's bad behavior and beliefs or damn them to Hell. You are with me or against me. Staking out a stark position and never deviating from it is viewed as clear thinking and righteousness.

To say this doesn't mean that nothing is clear or true. You can be sure that you are 100 percent right when you say racism, for example, is wrong. But I mean to remind us of the general complexity of life. Things are often not as simple as they seem, yet that doesn't mean they are never simple. You can see even here, how I am anticipating that many people will understand my writing about dualism in a dualistic manner. It's true *both* that most issues are complex *and* that some issues are very simple and clear. People, on the other hand, are inevitably extremely complex. We can name certain behaviors or beliefs as bad with moral clarity, but people—especially those we have never met—rarely will fit so neatly into a box.

As I came to learn, leaning too heavily on dualistic thinking makes offering grace to ourselves and others all but impossible.

The either/or framework keeps us in a graceless state where, as the Franciscan priest Richard Rohr told me, "everything remains in the world of equations, ledgers, measuring, weighing, counting, adding, subtracting."[2] It's a society where there are only two choices: punishment or celebration; accountability or zero consequences; loving people or hating their guts.

Dualistic thinking sets us against one another and creates toxic levels of conflict. It leads us to denounce wholesale people who disagree with us on political, ideological, or religious issues, because through the binary lens, a person could hold a differing view only because they are stupid, weak, craven, misinformed, selfish, or maybe even evil. Such thinking can leave us feeling perpetually annoyed by, angry at, or betrayed by people who don't share our point of view.

But beware: our brains have a cognitive bias toward binary thinking. This bias serves as a mental shortcut when a quick decision is needed, such as if our lives are in danger. But for nonurgent situations that require deeper analysis, it can obscure more nuanced options.[3] This tendency can be encouraged and reinforced by cultural norms.

Not all cultures exalt binary thinking. But Westerners have been steeped in binary logic. So, a person is either good or not good. Something is either true or not true.

It's not a coincidence that two of the major institutions in the United States that have driven so much of our conflict—the U.S. political system and white, Western Christianity—are inherently dualistic.

We are ruled by two political parties: Democratic and Republican. Yes, there are people who identify as independents, but there is no Independent party of any relevance and roughly 90 percent of those "independents" routinely tell pollsters they align with one of the two major parties.[4] What other choice do they have? If they don't throw in with a major party, many people reasonably feel they are effectively wasting their vote.

"America's relatively rigid, two-party electoral system stands apart [from other countries'] by collapsing a wide range of legitimate social and political debates into a singular battle line that can make our differences appear even larger than they may actually be," the Pew Research Center reported in late 2020. "When the balance of support for these political parties is close enough for either to gain near-term electoral advantage . . . the competition becomes cutthroat and politics begins to feel zero-sum, where one side's gain is inherently the other's loss. Finding common cause—even to fight a common enemy in the public health and economic threat posed by the coronavirus—has eluded us."[5]

The two-party system also creates the illusion that we can know who people are based on how they vote. For many voters, choosing to pull the lever for a particular candidate is often seen as going with the lesser of two evils, not as a hearty endorsement. Other times people are single-issue voters and they choose their candidate based only on their stance on a particular issue, not because they agree with them on all their positions. In countries with parliamentary systems, the same person who voted Democrat or Republican in the United States despite grave disagreements with the candidate would have the option to go with a party that more accurately reflects their worldview.

Even within the binary divisions of Democrat and Republican, people split into smaller opposing factions and pit themselves against one another. Moderates are treated with disgust by those who skew more politically right or left. They are called "DINOs" and "RINOs" (Democrat and Republican in name only) to signify their alleged mealy-mouthed affinity for accommodation. Moderates label the left and right "extremists" who don't understand how the "real world" works. The common thread through all of this is that many members of these groups cannot comprehend the possibility that a decent, thoughtful, and informed person could see the world differently than they do.

The most politically engaged among us are particularly inclined to adopt the "us vs. them" paradigm. While we may believe that deep philosophical beliefs undergird the political positions that lead to so much conflict, a study published in a late-2020 edition of *Science* magazine noted that partisans— people who identify with one of the two major parties—are often motivated less by "triumphs of ideas than [by] dominating the abhorrent supporters of the opposing party."[6]

Put simply: in today's America, most of us hate the other party more than we love our own. Social scientists call this "negative partisanship," and it has become a defining feature of American politics.[7]

Some of the dualistic division caused by leaders and influencers is driven by the cynical quest for high ratings, fame, power, and prosperity. But it's also the framework bred in our bones. While it's true the people amping up our outrage intuitively know that they will be rewarded with clicks, lucrative book contracts, and high ratings, they also likely believe that they have accurately cast the situation as one in which good people are pitted against bad people, simply because that's how many of us have been trained to think. Until our society comes to appreciate the limits of dualistic thinking, we're unlikely to experience any meaningful change in our fractured state of discourse or find relief from the constant anxiety, anger, and dissatisfaction all this conflict creates.

When I'm debating issues, I often find myself battling false binaries. Instead of arguing over these manufactured controversies, we would be wise to adopt a "both/and" framework. Let me give you some examples.

If someone protests police brutality, the response often is "You hate police officers." But it's possible to *both* respect police officers *and* want police officers who engage in misconduct or worse to be held accountable. When, in early 2021, Meghan Markle discussed her suicidal ideation and the racist treatment she experienced in the United Kingdom, conservatives thundered that it was impossible to believe someone of her privilege and wealth could have it so bad. But it's possible *both* to be rich and privileged *and* to experience racism and suicidal ideation. When protestors say "Black Lives Matter," some respond that "All Lives Matter." But the first sentence is not an either/or statement. It isn't "Only Black Lives Matter." It's a reminder that Black lives are as precious as white lives, a truth that unfortunately is not acknowledged by all.

If we got rid of false binaries, our public debate would become exponentially less maddening and more constructive overnight.

During the #MeToo awakening spurred by allegations against Hollywood mogul Harvey Weinstein and other abusers, I would sit on set and listen to colleagues tell me that the men who had been accused of sexual harassment could not be guilty because they knew these men to be good people, good fathers, or good friends. Both of these things can be true: a man can both be a good friend to you and sexually harass someone. But binary thinking makes people all good or all bad, which is simply not how things work. People and situations are complex and nuanced. Good people do bad things sometimes.

Dualistic thinking became especially dangerous during the coronavirus epidemic in the United States. A video created by the Internet celebrity JP Sears captured this mentality to satirical perfection. The self-described "conscious comedian" shared a parody video with his 700,000 Instagram followers titled "How the Media Wants You to Think."[8] It featured various Instagram wellness guru types faux-earnestly staring into the camera and sharing what it meant to be "brave" in the midst of a global pandemic. "Bravery is refusing to get together with my friends and family that I love," one man intoned in a syrupy voice. "Bravery is living in constant fear," a woman using the same tone shared. "I'm brave enough to live in never-ending terror of a virus," said another. And so it went for two minutes, until it ended with Sears standing on a city street, ripping off his mask, and telling viewers how he was in danger of being censored for not parroting the party line regarding Covid-19.

It was a parody video, but it captured the real view held by many in the United States that voluntarily putting a piece of cloth over your nose and mouth when you left your house to protect others from getting sick was the equivalent of "living in constant fear." There was no room for the reality that you could both take the pandemic seriously *and* not spend your waking hours balled up in the fetal position.

It also set up a paradigm where you could either "do as I'm told without questioning it," as one Instagrammer said, or immediately reject any information coming from medical experts. There was no room for the commonsense measures of mask wearing or social distancing to protect others from getting sick while they shopped for groceries or attended church. Instead, according to this line of thinking, the only reason anyone would take such a measure seriously was that they were an authority-worshipping robot or a mentally unstable hysteric. If I thought those were the only two choices, I probably wouldn't have worn a mask either.

My awareness of how hyperdualism had been distorting my thinking and bringing misery into my life began in mid-2017. In addition to my fury at what was happening in the political sphere, I was having a full-blown spiritual crisis.

In difficult times, I had turned to my faith to give me solace and to reorient me. But no matter how hard I tried, I simply couldn't bring my spiritual beliefs into alignment with my behavior or silence the chattering soundtrack of judgment and doom in my head. In fact, if I'm being totally honest, I didn't even *want* to bring them into alignment anymore.

"Love my enemies?" "Bless those who persecute you?" "Judge not, lest you be judged?"

No thanks.

God clearly didn't understand what was going on down here.

The truth is, I was at the end of my rope with Christianity and was sincerely doubting if wisdom could be found in a religion that had caused so much suffering for so many people, including me. I had left evangelicalism a few years before and turned to the Catholic Church, which was deeply rooted in my family's Irish Catholic history. The binary teaching and ethos of the evangelical churches I had attended had ultimately felt discordant with how I experienced God and understood the teachings of Jesus, and I had found solace in the liturgy and spiritual practices of the Catholic Church, even if I disagreed with some of the teachings.

I thought that I had found more nuance in the Catholic Church until one day I mentioned to my neighbor, a conservative Dominican priest, that I was dating a wonderful man who I thought might be "the one." "But you don't have an annulment for your marriage yet," he said, slightly panicked. He was referring to my divorce a few years earlier. "You need to break up with Robert until you have an annulment, because in God's eyes you are still married." I knew annulments could take years and could also be denied.

I started to panic. I had been waiting to meet someone like Robert my whole life. It was one thing to disagree with church teaching on homosexuality or women priests, as I did, but it was another thing to be violating teaching myself. As I'm writing these words, I find it impossible to get inside the head of the woman who was thinking these things and make it sound rational. All I can tell you is that I was completely locked into dualistic thinking. There were only two options: break up with Robert or leave the Catholic Church. I simply could not offer grace to myself to do anything less than perfectly.

I became so consumed with anxiety about this, I could barely function. I agonized over the issue for the next six months. I'm frankly surprised Robert didn't just break up with me. I had to go to a therapist who specialized in anxiety to try to get stabilized. "Why have you only spoken to a conservative priest about this, when you are not a conservative?" she asked, staring at me quizzically.

I sat in stunned silence. I had no answer. I now know that I only wanted advice from people who thought dualistically because I didn't trust people who didn't. Again, don't ask me to make sense of this, because I can't. Religious trauma had broken my brain.

As I would learn later, while most of us are inclined toward binary thinking, people who have experienced trauma can move into an extreme version of this perspective. It creates a sense of psychological safety but can utterly blind them to alternative ways of seeing. When a person is in this state, nuance or uncertainty can feel psychologically intolerable.

A year into this crisis, exhausted from the graceless emotional battering I had inflicted on myself because of my inability to be a "good Catholic," I was about to give up on the Catholic Church, and the entire Christian project. As I was on the verge of bolting, I serendipitously discovered the Franciscan priest and writer Richard Rohr and the Jesuit priest James Martin. Rohr is a bestselling author and teacher of contemplative Christianity with a large following that includes many people who have been harmed or alienated by religion. Martin is known to many for his recurring role as the "official chaplain" back in the days of *The Colbert Report,* in addition to his bestselling books and his advocacy for LGBTQIA people. This wise, brilliant, and gentle priest generously offered to be my spiritual director, probably signing up for more than he bargained for.

Rohr and Martin set me on the path toward a new understanding of grace, though it would be awhile before this entered my awareness. Reading Rohr's books and attending a small retreat with him in Santa Fe helped reorient me to the world, my faith, and even myself. Perhaps the most important notion that he planted in my brain was that I might not be seeing the world as clearly as I thought. He introduced me to non-dualism and showed me that life provides more options than aligning with one of two opposite extremes and how to create space for the "both/and" of life. This was radical thinking for me. I was being asked to undo a lifetime of seeing the world through the lens of good versus evil.

Through Rohr I learned about contemplative Christianity, which has deep roots in the Catholic Church but had been mostly lost to the Western Church. I started to practice centering prayer, in which you choose a sacred word or symbol, clear your mind, and sit for twenty minutes. This is ideally done twice a day. When your mind wanders, you pull it back to the sacred word or symbol you have chosen. It requires little more than sitting in God's presence and opening yourself up to the work of the Spirit of God. Over time, I began to notice a difference in how I reacted to what was happening around me. I felt more peace and clarity, and developed a growing tolerance for nuance.

But I was ten universes away from seeing the world this way when I showed up for my first meeting with Father Martin in May 2017. I was a bundle of anxiety and fear, which flowed directly from my existential crisis about my faith. In addition to "annulment-gate," I had become increasingly angry with the patriarchal structure of the Catholic Church and the abuse it spawned. I wanted women priests, like, yesterday. A new sexual abuse scandal had emerged, and I was spitting nails. I was unloading my grievances a mile a minute.

Martin needed to stabilize the patient first, and he did so by bringing me back to the basics with a simple question: "How do you feel when you are connected to God?"

My answer was simple: "Calm and at peace."

Then maybe all this anxiety isn't coming from God, Martin suggested.

I exhaled and felt calm for the first time in a really long time.

Father Martin became a master of breaking down my binary beliefs and steering me away from black-and-white interpretations of those with whom I disagreed, including the Catholic Church. He helped me see I didn't need to throw Jesus out with the bathwater. He reminded me that the Church taught I had a conscience and that I should pray and search my conscience for a way forward. There was no emergency: I didn't have to rush to discern the best path.

I could show myself some grace.

Father Martin gingerly began the process of pulling me back from the way I had learned to understand God in the evangelical church, where there seemed to be a preordained answer for nearly every issue. He introduced me to the importance of mystery in faith, of recognizing that I can't know everything. I started to grasp Saint Augustine's famous (and nondualistic) assertion about the mystery of the Divine, *"Si enim comprehendis, non est Deus"* or roughly "If you comprehend it, it is not God."[9]

I started to consider the reality that the Catholic Church is *both* patriarchal *and* contains deep wisdom, including the wisdom of women saints and theologians. I reminded myself that the Church is an evolving institution, which has changed through its thousands of years in existence and can change again. I could see it as a place that *both* has committed grave evil *and* is a critical voice and support for immigrants, migrants, the incarcerated, inmates on death row, universal health care, income equality, people living in poverty, and the fight against climate change.

It is also a place where I had deeply experienced the presence of God and that connects me to my Irish ancestors, who were sustained by their Catholic faith through many dangers, toils, and snares. It is the Church that was so integral to my beloved grandparents' lives that when their nonbelieving daughter refused to have their granddaughter baptized, they performed a secret emergency baptism of me at a Catholic Church while visiting, a fact they only disclosed a decade later. (The Catholic Church deemed this baptism valid during my annulment process.)

I began to understand the Church as a "self-surpassing community that transcends space and time, geography and millennia, past and future" that could not be defined by a "culture bound creation of an imperial government," as the hanging-on-by-a-thread Catholic author James Carroll has written.[10]

Rather than break with the Catholic Church because of all-or-nothing thinking, I began to wrestle with it. I entered liminal space—the in-between place where we are starting to leave one way of being for another, with no idea of where this process will lead.

As I learned more about my natural propensity for dualism, I began reflecting on how it had manifested in my life. It was stomach-churning stuff. My reign of certitude had been borne by friends, family, co-workers, and the occasional stranger at a cocktail party who made the mistake of suggesting *Chicago* was not the best musical in existence. When I became a Christian, it was like pouring gasoline on the fire. Adding the patina of religiosity to my beliefs only made me more certain about my righteousness. My private interactions were enormously regrettable and cringe inducing, but at least they were not on the public stage. As I came to reconsider past columns, tweets, and on-air interactions—proclamations for all the world to see—I began to experience pangs of guilt and embarrassment.

I realized I needed to change. But learning how to apply these lessons in the hyperdualistic world of media and politics would take some time.

Chapter 4

THE DEVIL YOU KNOW

People can't see what they can't see. Their biases get in the way,
surrounding them like a high wall, trapping them
in ignorance, deception, and illusion.
—Brian McLaren[1]

When I first moved to New York City after a decade in
Washington, DC, I was delighted to discover that almost
every person I met shared my ideological and political worldview. On the rare occasion I would bump into a Republican, I
would just back away slowly and seek out a more like-minded
companion.

I grew accustomed to the political homogeneity of the city
and never gave it much thought until late 2007, when I decided
to buy an apartment in the Chelsea neighborhood of Manhattan. I made a strong offer, and my agent assured me the apartment would be mine despite other bids. Instead of the smooth
sailing she promised, I received a panicked phone call. The
owners were wary about accepting my bid because I had recently started a job as a political analyst at Fox News. They felt
this might cause the co-op board to reject my application.

"I told them you were a Democrat," my agent explained.
"But they aren't convinced." The owners said the building had

a tight-knit community, and the co-op board didn't want to have people around who might make residents uncomfortable. Though I suspected the board's behavior might be illegal, I followed my agent's instructions and emailed links to my television appearances and columns to demonstrate my left-of-center bona fides. Thus reassured, they accepted my offer, and I moved in soon after.

During the two years I lived there, I became friends with the couple who lived across the hall and the woman who lived directly below me. But I never witnessed the tight-knit community that had been described to me. It was a small building, with three apartments per floor, so I rarely even saw my neighbors in the hallway. There was no area, like a roof deck or courtyard, where people gathered. There wasn't even a lobby. But even had there been, how disruptive would it really have been to make small talk with a Republican occasionally?

A year prior, I wouldn't have thought twice about the board's concern. For most of my time in New York, I had associated only with Democrats at work and in my personal life. But joining Fox News had put me in constant proximity to Republicans, and I had come to find that I actually liked some of them. I was surprised at how I would occasionally find agreement with them on certain issues, such as providing a pathway to citizenship for undocumented immigrants or opposing the Iraq War. They didn't match the one-dimensional caricature I had created about them, any more than I resembled the one-dimensional caricature they often used to describe Democrats in the abstract.

To be fair, the views of my apartment building's co-op board were on trend for the country. A few years before, Bill Bishop's book *The Big Sort* revealed how Americans had increasingly self-segregated into like-minded communities, a shift that fuels our contempt for the opposing side.[2]

In an analysis of the 2020 election, Bishop noted that while the national election was closely fought, almost 60 percent of voters lived in a county where one of the candidates won by a landslide.[3] That number was roughly 26 percent in 1976. The increasing political homogeneity of our communities can be comforting, but it can also goad us into believing that everyone thinks like us and that anyone who doesn't is a dummy or maybe even a bad person. By siloing ourselves, we have put ourselves mostly in the dark when it comes to really understanding our political and ideological opponents.

But that doesn't stop us from forming strong opinions about each other.

In June 2019, a More in Common survey found that 86 percent of Republicans described Democrats as brainwashed, and 84 percent said they were hateful.[4] The disdain was mutual. Eighty-eight percent of Democrats described Republicans as "brainwashed," and 87 percent found them hateful.

There's nothing wrong with disagreeing on issues. It's not a problem to feel angry at people who hold views you believe are harmful. Trouble arises when people hold members of the opposing political party in absolute contempt. We are "othering" people and making judgments about the fundamental decency of people we have never met based on a single piece of information: their political identity. This alienation from people who hold opposing views has implications for our ability to see our fellow citizens through the lens of grace and drives the polarization that causes so much dysfunction when it comes to governing and trying to solve the nation's problems.

One of the most troubling aspects of partisan politics and adherence to ideological identities is how they can lead to dehumanization of the "other." As recounted in the *Atlantic,* when New York University researcher Jay Van Bavel "looks at the brain scans [of study participants], he finds that the brain regions used to empathize with others aren't as active when a person is evaluating faces he or she has been told belong to the other team."[5] If we have trouble showing empathy when nothing is at stake, imagine how dangerous this tendency can be once we add strong ideological, political, or religious views to the mix.

Since we spend most of our time with people who think like us, how do we form such strong opinions about our opponents?

Unfortunately, we are forced to rely on the media and our like-minded friends on social media who share stories that reinforce what we already believe. By avoiding contact with people who are different from us, we make ourselves much more susceptible to other people's narratives about them, which are rarely benign. We are also left with the impression that the people dominating the airwaves, opinion pages, and social media are representative of most Americans. But the average American is not as ideologically pure or partisan as the people driving our national debate.

Furthermore, we are at the mercy of the unconscious biases of our brains. The psychologist and meditation teacher Tara Brach explained in a 2019 talk that our brain's quick sorting mechanism can cause us to engage in "bad othering," especially when we are under duress or have unprocessed trauma.[6] We engage in bad othering when we feel anger and disgust for other people, which often leads us to hold them in contempt. "For millions of years, 'what could go wrong' to our humanoid hunter-gatherer groups was other hunter-gatherer groups that were slightly different, or greatly different than us," Brach explained. In this context, different equaled danger.

Many of us might insist that all our opposition is based only on reason. "Well, I despise the other side because they hold terrible beliefs and support terrible policies. We have nothing in common." Academic research does not support this contention. A *Science* magazine paper "Political Sectarianism in America" noted, "Overall, the severity of political conflict has grown increasingly divorced from the magnitude of policy disagreement."[7]

Studies have shown that the information we rely on to fuel our hatred of the other side often isn't an accurate representation of what they believe. The authors of the More in Common survey found there was a huge "perception gap" among partisans, creating a deeply distorted understanding between people in opposing political camps. Overall, "Democrats and Republicans imagine that almost twice as many people on the other side hold extreme views than really do," the survey found.[8]

Democrats estimated that about half of Republicans believe "properly controlled immigration can be good for America." In reality, 85 percent of Republicans agreed with this idea. Republicans thought that 45 percent of Democrats believed that it's important men have protection from false accusations of sexual assault, when in fact 74 percent of Democrats agreed with that sentiment.[9]

A 2018 study found that Americans believed that 32 percent of Democrats are LGBT (lesbian, gay, bisexual, and transgender) when in fact it's 6 percent. They also believed that 38 percent of Republicans earn over $250,000 per year, when it's actually 2 percent.[10]

Because people tend to have distorted views of what members of the political parties actually believe, being exposed to real people might be a good way to cut down on polarization and stem the tide of dehumanizing attitudes about the "other." This is doubly true if you are interested in trying to bring grace into our raging dumpster fire of a culture.

Bowling Green State University philosophy professor Kevin Vallier, author of the 2020 book *Trust in a Polarized Age,* told me in an interview that he sees institutional policy fixes to some of our polarization, but views much of this battle as a heart issue. He suggests we do some heart examination, asking ourselves two related questions. "The first one is, do we even want to trust our political opponents? Do we even care about trusting them?" he says. "The second question is, are we even interested in seeing them as people of goodwill? Because if we aren't, we can't change the problem."[11]

This is obviously a hard one for a lot of people who've written off broad swaths of society as irredeemably hopeless causes. A baby step to take here might be to consider the possibility that, even if you believe most of your political opponents are people of bad will, there are some who are not.

It's true that there are some people—specifically certain political, ideological, and religious leaders—who are transparently not acting in good faith. They have agendas that have nothing to do with informing others or working for the common good, and everything to do with preserving or expanding their power or pocketbooks. We are not expected to pretend that they are doing anything but looking out for their own very narrow interests. But I've found it's rare to find a private person who expresses beliefs as an act of bad faith. I'm sure they exist, but usually their problematic, false, and harmful beliefs can be traced directly to a toxic news source or leader.

Sometimes I hear people say that they are watching or reading "the other side's" news sources in an effort to be more balanced or see things from the other side's point of view. However, this practice can backfire. Computational social scientist Chris Bail found that when he showed people content from the other end of the political spectrum, it just made them more committed to their existing positions. But being exposed to *actual people* from the other side can be beneficial. When Bail put anonymous users on a social media platform in conversation with a person who held opposing political views, people became less polarized.[12]

In fact, just one conversation with a person from the opposing party has been shown to tamp down hostility. "We found that a 15-minute, in-person conversation with members of the other party dramatically reduced partisan hostility relative to those who only talked to others from their own party," wrote researchers Matthew Levendusky and Dominik Stecula in a January 2021 op-ed.[13] They noted that the participants were surprised by how much they enjoyed the exercise and the fact that they could find common ground with someone from an opposing party.

This doesn't mean that people who hold opposing views or values need to be your best friends—though they could be. Perhaps the most famous example of a political odd-couple friendship is that of two lions of the Supreme Court: liberal icon Ruth Bader Ginsburg and conservative giant Antonin Scalia. They regularly dined and vacationed together, and their families often gathered to ring in the New Year together.[14]

"What's not to like? Except her views on the law," Scalia once quipped.[15] Ginsburg wrote that she and Scalia were long-time "best buddies," noting that his dissents on her draft opinions "nailed all the weak spots" and always made the final versions of the opinions better.[16] Ginsburg explained at her dear friend's memorial service, "He was once asked how we could be friends given our disagreements on lots of things. Justice Scalia answered: 'I attack ideas. I don't attack people. Some very good people have some very bad ideas.'"[17]

Certainly no one would argue that their differences were rare or shallow. An analysis of closely decided 5–4 cases in 2012 found that Scalia and Ginsburg agreed just 7 percent of the time. Their vigorous debates and disagreements had real-world consequences that few of us will ever encounter in our relationships. Scalia and Ginsburg's disagreements were over some of the most hotly contested issues of our day, from same-sex marriage to gender equality to abortion rights, and their opinions shaped the legal system of the United States.

One of Scalia's former law clerks, Jeffrey Sutton, recalled a conversation during one of his last visits with his former boss. Scalia pointed to two dozen roses and said he needed to take them to "Ruth" for her birthday. Sutton asked him, "What good have all these roses done for you? Name one 5–4 case of any significance where you got Justice Ginsburg's vote." Scalia replied, "Some things are more important than votes."[18]

This relationship could not have existed but for grace. Embedded in their friendship was an appreciation and love for each other that transcended political, ideological, or religious beliefs. It transcended many of the same issues that are currently ripping this country apart at the seams.

My closest friends align with me ideologically and politically. Of course, we don't agree on everything, but when we look at the world, or the problems of our country, we see basically the same things. Our disagreements are on the fringes. But that doesn't mean I don't have any people in my life who believe radically different things than I do.

I still have friends from my evangelical Christian days whom I love. I have remained friends with some of the Republicans I worked with at Fox News as well. I have conservative Catholics in my life with whom I have huge disagreements about theological and political issues, but I still cherish those relationships. None of these people voted for Trump, but my sister-in-law's parents, whom I absolutely adore, not only voted for him— they *love* him. I've tried to talk them out of it, but I lost that battle. (They're not crazy about my worldview either, for what it's worth.)

While watching a contentious 2019 Capitol Hill hearing, I almost fell out of my chair when I heard Democratic Rep. Elijah Cummings say that GOP Rep. Mark Meadows, a key Trump ally and one of the most conservative members of Congress, was one of his best friends. Cummings later told the *Washington Post,* "We need to get away from party and deal with each other as human beings."[19] This echoes a point made by Vallier, that "we need nonpolitical identities that are crosscutting with our political identities." So, my nonpolitical identities that crosscut with people of vastly different political views would be my Catholic faith or belonging to the same family.[20]

When Cummings passed away later that year, Meadows tearfully eulogized him. As mind-blowing as this relationship was to me, the truth is, there are many political oddball friendships in Washington. It's the nature of being forced to work with people who are radically different from you. You get to experience them as full human beings, not just as their political identity.

It's important to note that these kinds of friendships aren't for everyone. Some people just don't have the energy or bandwidth. For others, it can feel demeaning or emotionally unsafe to engage in such relationships. Having a conversation with a political or ideological opponent can decrease hostility for some people, but for others it might result in increased animosity. So, everyone needs to determine their own limitations and set their own boundaries. But for those who are interested in bridge building, these kinds of relationships are crucial to slowing the warp speed at which we are sorting ourselves away from our fellow Americans.

Members of marginalized communities understandably can feel betrayed when they see a person they admire engaging with someone who holds harmful views about people like them. For example, in early 2020, Christian writer Jen Hatmaker received blowback from her audience when she interviewed non-LGBTQIA-affirming Christian leaders on her podcast. In a Facebook post, Hatmaker explained her thinking and reaffirmed her commitment to loving and supporting LGBTQIA people: "For years, several progressive faith leaders and a few LGBTQ folks held a door open for me before I was meaningfully engaged in the work of justice, before I was [LGBTQ] affirming . . . they made room for the process of evolving. Because they didn't shame or exclude me . . . I felt safe to listen and learn, to ask hard questions. They gave me the gift of time.

They gave me the gift of many discussions around other shared ideas . . . There is no way to explain how much this mattered to my growth. I will be grateful forever." She noted that if she had been shut out "by progressive leaders and their communities even five years ago, I cannot imagine where I would be."[21]

Hatmaker was highlighting a basic truth: when we engage with people rather than shaming them, they very well may come to see that they are in error about an important issue. It's also worth noting that she is talking about leaders, not just your average person. Leaders better serve their mission if they can engage with people who don't support their cause, because politics and activism are about addition, not subtraction. Hatmaker further explained that she felt called to be a bridge builder for LGBTQIA issues so that members of that community wouldn't have to carry that burden alone.

But people who aren't in leadership positions can play bridge-building roles in their own spheres of influence. This is what it means to be an ally. It's important to have the hard conversations with the people in your life about racism, misogyny, and other forms of bigotry. At the same time, everyone needs to create space for bridge builders to do this work and not attack them or shame them for having relationships with people from opposing political or ideological camps. We all have different roles to play in the world. Just because someone else is approaching social change in a different way than you might doesn't make it automatically wrong. (Remember, that's dualistic thinking.)

Lest you think I'm suggesting you go befriend a person for the purposes of converting them to your views, let me be clear: it is not okay to engage in friendship fraud. Genuine relationships are built on mutual respect, not the premise that you need to save another person from their terrible beliefs. How would you feel if you found out someone did this to you?

Justices Scalia and Ginsburg vigorously argued with one another, but there is no evidence they engaged in the friendship with the goal of converting the other's worldview. "They liked to fight things out in good spirit—in fair spirit—not the way we see debates these days on television," NPR's Supreme Court reporter Nina Totenberg recalled after Scalia's death.[22] Instead they focused on the things they loved: opera, their hometown of New York City, and their families.

Growing up in a fiercely Democratic family, I heard plenty of demonization of Republicans at our dinner table. It was just second nature. I don't think we ever stopped to consider if what we were saying was actually true. My professor parents believed Republicans were anti-intellectual, racist, selfish, and indifferent to the poor. Except, of course, the ones with whom we were friendly.

Living in Alaska, we were surrounded by Republicans. If one of our Ronald Reagan–loving neighbors knocked on the door to borrow a cup of sugar, my mother could segue from a rant against Reaganomics to warmly greeting said neighbor and inviting them in for coffee. Cognitive dissonance would take over.

When we hold two competing views, it creates psychological discomfort for us. To restore a sense of balance, we will either abandon one of the beliefs or find a way to make both of them true, even if it makes no sense. Our brains engage in an unconscious process that social scientists call "motivated reasoning," whereby we decide what we believe and then search for reasons to support or justify that belief.[23]

My mother could not believe that Republicans were terrible, immoral people *and* believe that the lovely Republican neighbor who generously watched my brother and me whenever my mother was late coming home from work was a good person. In the moment, my mother would forget the harsh generalizations and see a real person who was more than the sum of her political beliefs. If someone had pressed her on the discrepancy later, she would have dismissed it by saying, "Joanna is different."

Let's be clear: the belief systems that separated my family and most of our fellow townsfolk were not minor. My family disagreed with our neighbors on a spate of important issues including affirmative action, gender equality, and gay rights. While Reagan was revered in the town in which we lived, my mother *despised* him. I don't know if there was a single evening when she didn't hurl an expletive or cooking utensil at the television if he came on.

By high school, when I started having political conversations, I could find nobody who thought the way I did. I owe my debating skills mostly to my family's dinner-table throwdowns over politics, but those skills were further honed by sparring constantly with one of my teenage besties, Carrie, who—like nearly every person in my tiny Jesuit high school—came from a staunchly Republican family.

We started our arguments as passionate fourteen-year-olds, continued our debates as college roommates, then took them to Capitol Hill, where we shared a house after college. She worked for a Republican senator, and I worked for a Democratic fundraising firm. Later, I would talk to her on the phone from my office in the Clinton administration while she sat in her office at the conservative think tank, the Heritage Foundation. Our conversations typically were debates over what we'd read in the newspaper that morning, particularly whatever we saw on the op-ed page. It's remarkable how unremarkable this was at the time, because we disagreed on pretty much everything. We drifted apart as we got older but remain friends, grabbing coffee now and then and sometimes having Christmas dinner together when we are in town at the same time.

Unlike my family in Alaska, most people are not interacting regularly with people who hold dramatically different political views. They are more like I was when I first moved to New York City, thriving in an echo chamber.

While many of us cluster into like-minded groups, researchers have found that more than 80 percent of Americans say they know someone from the other party that they like and respect.[24] This person might be a co-worker or neighbor who isn't necessarily a friend or perhaps it's a relative you see only once or twice a year. When researchers ask study participants to think about such a person (versus an abstract Republican or Democrat), they start to depolarize.[25]

Thinking about a person you know and like who belongs to the opposing political party or is aligned with an ideological camp you despise can be a quick tool to ground you when a social media post or news report sends you down the road of furious demonization and "othering" of broad swaths of people you don't know. It can depolarize you and help you remember that people are more complex than the one-dimensional way we typically portray members of political parties or ideological factions.

Rather than believing that a co-worker or neighbor is the exception to the rule for people in the opposing party, we might consider treating them like the norm. Chances are, we haven't found a unicorn. There are probably others out there who we would appreciate if we got to know them.

Using grace as our touchstone, we might just be surprised what happens when we open our minds and hearts to people who are different from us.

Chapter 5

WHEN GRACE RUNS OUT

One doesn't have to operate with great malice to do great harm.
The absence of empathy and understanding are sufficient.

—CHARLES M. BLOW[1]

While God's grace is unlimited, here on earth humans have their breaking point.

If you take advantage of someone's grace over and over, you shouldn't be surprised when you discover their patience has reached its expiration date. If you refuse to empathize with, or listen to, a person or group of people, and they get tired of repeatedly explaining something to you, you may eventually suffer harsh consequences.

If this happens, it's your fault, not theirs. They are not denying you grace; they are holding you accountable.

Most of us have been in a relationship where someone has pushed things past the point of no return. We may have been the perpetrator or we may have been the victim. You tell your husband repeatedly that his close contact with female co-workers makes you feel disrespected. He tells you that you are too sensitive and need to stop acting like such a victim. You aren't going to get divorced over this, so you offer him grace and try to move on.

But your husband continues to text and grab drinks with single women in the office. You tell him again how you feel. This time you raise your voice, and he tells you that he doesn't like your "tone." He makes some vague comment about cutting back on his contact, even though according to him you are exaggerating the problem. This cycle repeats itself with you getting increasingly angry, maybe even screaming at him as he again references your "tone" and calls you "out of control." You suggest that the two of you do a couples workshop, and he mockingly rolls his eyes. Maybe you bring him a book to read about how couples can communicate better. He waves you off dismissively.

After this cycle repeats too many times, after the grace you have extended for years has been abused repeatedly, you reach your breaking point. One night you find him texting with a young woman at the office and you tell him the relationship is over. "What? Why?" he wails. "Give me another chance!" You're being unfair, giving him the death penalty for one mistake. But it's not one mistake. You have been telling him for years that what he is doing is hurtful to you. You have cried over this—perhaps many times. He has seen you suffer, but your suffering hasn't moved him to have empathy for you or do the work to make your relationship better. So you file for divorce and he acts injured and blindsided. He's back to calling you crazy for your "overreaction."

Does this remind you of anything?

Because it's similar to the dynamic of Black people trying to get white people to take racism—and in particular, police brutality—seriously and treat it like the house-on-fire crisis that it is. It has echoes of the dynamic faced by women who were largely ignored when they worked to create a culture that takes sexual assault and harassment seriously, or by LGBTQIA people who had to fight, and continue to fight, for their right to be treated with dignity and as full citizens. Really, it sounds like pretty much every marginalized group that has been asking since the beginning of time for people to hear their cries and do something about the issues they are raising.

How have their demands that we treat them with basic equality been answered? They have been ignored, called crazy, put off, told to wait, accused of imagining or exaggerating their situation, and admonished for being too shrill or aggressive in their complaints. In the face of sufficient pressure, the people in power might assume a posture resembling sympathy or promise things will get better. And perhaps they'll offer remedies around the margins. There might be some marginal improvement. But the underlying problems don't go away.

Of course, the experience of people who belong to marginalized groups is exponentially worse than the disagreement between the wife and husband, since after all, the wife is not arguing over her basic humanity. Plus, she can divorce this jerk and find someone else. People from marginalized groups never had this option. To the extent we have seen change, it only really began in a serious way when it was made intolerable for people to ignore these groups any longer. The Me Too and Black Lives Matter movements made it an imperative that organizations and businesses start listening and start holding people accountable or pay the reputational or financial consequences. Other marginalized groups have adopted similar tactics, recognizing that the way to get Americans to really care about an issue is to hit them where it hurts: in the pocketbook.

It would have been preferable if people just listened in the first place and were driven by empathy and concern for their fellow humans, not by the bottom line or career preservation. But they weren't, and indeed many still are offended at the idea that people are being held accountable for harmful behavior.

"Why are you canceling people?" they demand to know. "Why are you overreacting to this one thing?"

What about grace?

So much grace has been extended—and for so long. But at some point, a grace period ends. You can be late with your mortgage payment by a week, but you can't be late by a month, or there will be a late fee. After three months, your mortgage could be canceled and you might even lose your house. So it is with issues that have been explained ad nauseam, for generations, to people who have refused to listen.

The grace period for racism, misogyny, and all bigotry is over. I didn't decide that. I'm merely observing reality. The widespread toleration, if not outright celebration, of so much toxic, abusive, and dehumanizing behavior never should have occurred. But it did. We have now belatedly arrived at the point in our country's history where people can decide if they want to keep being part of the problem or start becoming part of the solution.

We are past the time when a white person should reasonably expect that saying the N-word is not going to have serious repercussions. No longer should any man be surprised that if he sexually harasses a woman, the weight of the world will come down on him. Grown people who go on Twitter and treat trans people like garbage need to stop acting surprised when people don't want to associate with them or buy their products anymore.

When these things happen, people cry "cancel culture" and demand grace for the person who has caused the harm. But what if we had grace for the people who have been pushed not just to the brink, but over the edge, by disregard, disrespect, and worse?

"To live in this country as part of a marginalized community is to feel constantly under assault," the writer and antiracism leader Lisa Sharon Harper told me.[2] "It is to be the target of graceless attacks against one's bodies, family, and future. It is a form of warfare that comes through our politics, policy, and microaggressions at work and in society."

We are always hearing about how white people need grace for using racial slurs, how heterosexual people need grace for using homophobic slurs, and how men need grace for making sexually inappropriate comments. But the exact same people making these demands don't offer a drop of grace to people who have been telling us what a decent society looks like since the beginning of time. No, they call them "snowflakes" or sneer about "social justice warriors (SJWs)" or call their peaceful protests unpatriotic or terroristic. Do people really think that marginalized people haven't noticed what a one-way street grace is?

What if we put the responsibility for so-called cancel culture where it belongs—on a society that refuses to change or listen until it literally has no other choice?

Indeed, the idea of "cancellation" was conceived by Black Twitter as a tactic to get people with power to listen to their concerns. "Being canceled . . . should be read as a last-ditch appeal for justice," wrote University of Virginia professor Meredith D. Clark in a 2020 academic paper.[3] Cancellation is "an expression of agency, a choice to withdraw one's attention from someone or something whose values, (in)action, or speech are so offensive, one no longer wishes to grace them with their presence, time, and money."

Cancellation was primarily "reserved for celebrities, brands, and otherwise out-of-reach figures," Clark noted. It was sometimes as simple as unfollowing a person on social media and ceasing to purchase their products, and other times operated as a more formal attempt to gain accountability by pushing "the ever-present issue of everyday racism to the top of the news media's agenda" through hashtag-driven discussion of issues such as white people calling the police on Black people who had done nothing wrong.[4]

Perhaps predictably, the creative and empowering cancellation tactic mutated as it was adopted by social elites online. It is now used on public and private citizens alike, who are often reduced to one-dimensional beings, viewed as only the offensive thing they did or said. Dr. Clark notes, "The noise of online harassment, doxxing, and bad-faith piling on [now] drowns out Black Twitter's approach toward demanding accountability in digital spaces."[5]

Somewhere along the line "cancellation" turned into "cancel culture"—a phrase that means so many different things to different people that it has been rendered meaningless. At one end of the spectrum, it's described as a way for "woke monsters" to destroy people's lives because their fragile sensibilities have been offended. At the other end, people say cancel culture is a figment of the imagination and invoked only by people who don't want powerful people to be held accountable.

It's a little more complicated than that, but one thing is undeniable: white people have appropriated the terms *cancellation* and *woke* from Black culture and twisted their meanings to weaponize them against Black people and people from other marginalized groups who are tired of being disrespected, demonized, or dehumanized. It's interesting that it is rarely deemed "cancel culture" when white conservatives get people fired for offending them.

The phrase "cancel culture" flattens every instance of calls for accountability for racist, sexist, or other bigoted behavior; ignores other factors at play; and inevitably presents the story like this: Nice (usually) white person is just going about their business. They say something that upsets the "snowflakes." Within minutes, they are out on the street without a job and with their reputation in tatters.

The implication is always: *you or your children are next.*

This is not to suggest that under the rubric of cancel culture—no matter how cynically and hypocritically some people wield it—there are no examples of people being publicly humiliated, defenestrated, and banished from the Kingdom in a way that feels more like annihilation than accountability. But often there is more nuance and backstory about the incidents that consume our news cycles than most people are led to believe. In addition to the specifics of each incident, always hovering in the background is the metastory of a culture that ignores the complaints of marginalized people until it is forced to care. It's a place where marginalized people have been expected to serve as bottomless containers of grace for people who by all appearances don't care much about them or what they think.

One of the biggest cancel culture stories of 2021 demonstrates how so many of these incidents are oversimplified to fit the narrative that the woke want to feast on your mutilated carcass. In 2019, Donald McNeil, a white *New York Times* reporter, was asked by a student in a group of teenagers on a *NYT*-sponsored trip whether he thought a white student should've been suspended for using the "N-word." He said it depended on the context, and his response included saying the full word. The teenagers were offended, complaints were made, and no apology proffered from McNeil because he didn't think he did anything wrong.

When the issue went public about a year later in the form of a *Daily Beast* article, the *New York Times* asked him to issue this statement: "My comments were offensive and I should not have made them, and I apologize." He refused, explaining in an email, "I do not feel I said or did anything offensive. This makes it sound like I targeted someone with a racial slur. I did not."

McNeil was told repeatedly by editors at the *Times* that his remarks were offensive, regardless of his intent. So he reached out to Dean Baquet, the *Times*'s executive editor and a friend, to intervene. Baquet, who is Black, replied: "But, Donald, it was dumb and whether you meant it to be that way or not it was insensitive." McNeil ultimately relented when he realized his job was on the line, but it was too late. Baquet later explained to him that word had spread that he refused to apologize, and he had "lost the newsroom." Too many people didn't want to work with him anymore. He was asked to resign.

How do I know all of this? Because McNeil chronicled the incident in a four-part series on *Medium* that was meant to demonstrate how unfairly he was treated but actually made his behavior seem even more problematic than its portrayal in the media coverage.[6]

McNeil did not lose his job for not realizing that non-Black people saying the N-word was offensive, even if it wasn't used as a slur. His resignation was the consequence of his inability to acknowledge that it was offensive once it was brought to his attention and apologize to the people he had offended. Essentially, he was asked to show some respect to his co-workers and consider that maybe he wasn't the judge and jury of whether it's okay for non-Black people to say the N-word, no matter the context. He was asked to be considerate and he refused. Personally, it's hard for me to imagine a situation where I could expect to keep my job after defying a request from my boss to apologize for offending fellow employees about anything, let alone using a racial slur, and harming the reputation of my workplace.

A few weeks after McNeil resigned, the *New York Times* reported that Mike Pesca, a well-known podcast host at the online publication *Slate,* had been suspended indefinitely. Pesca, who is white, had made the argument on the interoffice messaging platform Slack that there were some instances where it was okay for a non-Black person to use this word.[7] The anti–"cancel culture" crew were enraged that Pesca was punished, believing that the "woke mob" had struck again against a hapless man who just didn't know that there were people who found it offensive when non-Black people used the N-word, even if it wasn't being directed at someone as a slur.

Except Pesca had reportedly been confronted about this

exact behavior in the past.[8] "Mr. Pesca explored the argument over the use of the slur in a 2019 podcast about a Black security guard who was fired for using it," reported the *New York Times*.[9] When recording the episode, he made one with the slur and one without. His supervisor objected to the quotation of the slur, and the final episode did not include it. One would think that at this point Pesca would have realized something that most people already know: there are many people who don't appreciate hearing a white person use this word or debate about when it's okay to use the N-word.[10]

According to the online publication *Defector,* which obtained images of the Slack conversation, a Black staff writer inter-rupted the debate between Pesca and other staffers who were not Black, saying, "Feel like it's weird that everyone's dancing around the point that working in an environment where white people feel empowered to say the n-word in service of what-ever argument they want to make is incredibly hostile for black people."[11] This would have been a great place to stop and apol-ogize. Instead, according to *Defector,* Pesca summed up his po-sition this way: "There are some limited reasons why a non African American journalist or professor to use the word when conveying a quote in the name of clarity or factualness [*sic*]."[12]

In what seems like the understatement of the year, Joel An-derson, a Black staff member at *Slate,* told the *New York Times:* "For Black employees, it's an extremely small ask to not hear that particular slur and not have to debate about whether it's OK for white employees to use that particular slur."[13] I would add that there are many non-Black people who also find this behavior offensive, regardless of context.

Look, I get no joy out of people losing their jobs, no matter the circumstances. But if people want to plug their ears, cover their eyes, and ignore complaints from those who are being harmed, then nobody should be surprised when so-called can-cellations happen. Sometimes, though, children end up paying

the price for our culture's commitment to not learning or em-
pathizing with their fellow citizens.

In late 2020, the *New York Times* ran a story that inflamed
Conservative Twitter.[14] After receiving her learner's permit, a
white fifteen-year-old freshman girl had shared a video with a
friend via Snapchat saying, "I can drive, N——." The video
was circulated but didn't cause any controversy. Years later,
when the white teenager was a senior, someone shared the
video with a Black teenage boy in her class. When the white
teenager expressed her outrage about the murder of George
Floyd on social media, the Black teenage boy confronted her
online about the video. The accused girl said she was horrified
that she had ever used that word, and a Black girlfriend said she
had apologized to her for saying that word before the video
went viral.

A social media pile-on commenced and pressure was put on
the University of Tennessee, where the teenage girl had been
admitted as a student member of their top-rated cheer team.
The university asked her to withdraw. The teenage boy told the
New York Times that he and other Black students had complained
about the frequent use of the N-word by white kids at their
school. The teachers and principal did nothing, he said. He outlined other situations that had made Black students feel mistreated. In the end, the boy said he felt justified in what he did
because he "taught someone a lesson." He went on to college,
while the teenage girl was living at home and attending a local
community college.

I'll admit that when the teenage boy said he felt good about
the outcome because he "taught someone a lesson," my heart
sank. Where did he get the idea that people deserve to be
shown no mercy and punished severely even when they are
sorry? Perhaps he's noticed what happens when people like
him make mistakes. After all, as the *New York Times* noted, students of color faced "disproportionate disciplinary measures

compared with white students." He also, by all accounts, had been pushed to the edge by the way the school had ignored complaints of racism.

One journalist at the libertarian magazine *Reason* complained that the *New York Times* had even covered this story, "which concerns bad but by no means uncommon teenager behavior."[15] This was a fairly common sentiment among white reporters, mostly libertarian and conservative. Outraged over what had happened to this girl, they cast the use of the N-word by a white student as a dumb but unremarkable incident. "If [the female teenager] had cheated on her math test or planted a kick-me sign on a rival's back, would this constitute national news?" asked the writer.

The *Reason* article acknowledged complaints by Black students at the school—referring to them as "alleged unpleasantness"—and linked to a report that grew out of an investigation of the school district.[16] The report described behavior that went well beyond "unpleasantness," including complaints of "pervasive use of racial slurs and insults directed at students of color." The report noted the shocking "extent to which students report the use of the N-word as the prevailing concern and consistently discussed among students in the school environment" and that "the vast majority of the racial insults come from White students, White teachers, and White parents."

While railing against the injustice of this teenage girl's life being taken seriously off track for her having used a racial slur when she was fifteen, conservatives and libertarians viciously attacked the Black teenager, with one conservative journalist with a huge following declaring him a "moral monster" and the *National Review* labeling him "vindictive" in a headline. There was endless outrage about how the teenage girl was treated, but none could be spared to blast the hostile environment the Black teenager had described.

If the teachers and principal of the school had been doing

their jobs and keeping Black students safe from racist behavior at their school, maybe the Black teenager would not have felt he needed to do something to draw attention to the problem of white students saying the N-word. Maybe he wouldn't have felt like he needed to teach anyone a lesson if the teachers and principal had been teaching the lessons that these students clearly needed. If they had been holding students accountable for racist behavior, it's highly unlikely this boy would have felt pushed to do what he did.

"A riot," Rev. Dr. Martin Luther King Jr. said, "is the language of the unheard." In many ways, so are the tactics of cancellation.

What makes this story difficult is that it involves a teen who was severely shamed and punished for something she did four years earlier. Have you been around a fifteen-year-old lately? Would you survive the scrutiny if we had video of what you said when you were that age? This doesn't mean that teenagers shouldn't be held accountable, but the teenager in this situation got a good deal more than that. She suffered a severe public shaming, lost out on going away to college, and, thanks to the magic of the Internet, will forever be associated with something she did when she was fifteen.

At the same time, there are many Black fifteen-year-olds who would be happy if this was the worst thing that ever happened to them. Black children's lives are routinely destroyed without white people treating it as a crisis. They get kicked out of school for behavior their white counterparts only get a slap on the wrist for. The lack of grace shown to them can lead to their education and future being literally canceled. They get tried as adults for crimes even though they are children, and we don't see cancel culture obsessives rage-tweeting about that.

This is the point that someone will say, "But the solution isn't to give white children overly harsh punishments; it's to stop giving overly harsh punishments to Black children. We should be giving Black children the same grace white children routinely receive."

A wonderful vision. But when does that happen?

If we are willing to get honest with ourselves, when most white people make this statement, it's just a talking point. Until fairly recently, I made this argument with no awareness of how empty these words really were. This is a theoretical argument white people make to justify the deep concern, if not frantic fury, they feel when they see one white teenager having her college dreams snatched away. But we will then take zero steps to protect Black children from the systemic, ongoing abuse they receive at the hands of our school and criminal justice systems. We need to bring the same energy we have for the white teenage girl to all the Black children who regularly have their futures snatched away and dreams deferred.

We have a culture where conservatives treat the "cancellation" of cartoon figures and children's toys—Pepé Le Pew, books by Dr. Seuss, and Mr. and Mrs. Potato Head—as a national crisis. (Only one was actually canceled, or as it used to be known, discontinued. Pepé Le Pew's stalking and groping of female animated creatures didn't age well.) Conservatives have expressed more outrage about the fact that children will no longer be able to read Dr. Seuss books that refer to (and depict) Asians with "eyes at a slant" or portray Africans as monkeys than they ever have expressed about anti-Black or anti-Asian racism.

Many of the people who rail the most against "cancel culture" support or enable Donald Trump, who in 2019 refused to apologize for advocating that five Black and Latino teenagers accused of sexually assaulting and violently beating a Central Park jogger receive the death penalty. It was proven they were wrongly convicted, but not before they spent time in prison. *These were children*. Further, Donald Trump has never withdrawn his contention that boys as young as fourteen and fifteen should be put to death if found guilty of sexual assault, a crime of which Trump himself has been accused.[17]

We can acknowledge that many of the so-called cancel culture controversies are manufactured or based on half-truths or the belief that people shouldn't be punished for the kinds of behavior in which McNeil or Pesca engaged. But sometimes online culture does spin out of control; people can find themselves in the social media crosshairs over a single mistake, and no amount of apologizing can unshatter their lives. People can lose jobs for mistakes for which they are sorry and want to atone. They might find themselves unemployed for views they no longer hold. I will discuss these kinds of situations in more depth in the next chapter, but the backdrop for this conversation should always be considering why people sometimes feel they have to resort to these tactics.

It reminds me of something Clark Neily, a vice president for criminal justice at the libertarian Cato Institute, wrote about looting and rioting following the murder of George Floyd. "Before you can fairly assess the legitimacy of the ongoing protests or the quality of the government's response, you must understand the relevant facts," he said, addressing right-leaning people with whom he was typically otherwise ideologically aligned. "And the most relevant fact is that America's criminal justice system is rotten to its core. Though that certainly does not justify the violence and wanton destruction of property perpetrated by far too many protesters, it does provide useful context for comprehending the intensity of their anger and the fecklessness of the government's response. If America is burning, it is fair to say that America's criminal justice system—which is itself a raging dumpster fire of injustice—lit the fuse."[18]

About six months before he was assassinated, Rev. Dr. Martin Luther King Jr. told an audience of social scientists, "Urban riots are a special form of violence. They are not insurrections. The rioters are not seeking to seize territory or to attain control of institutions. *They are mainly intended to shock the white community.* Alienated from society and knowing that this society cherishes property above people, [the rioter] is shocking it by abusing property rights" (italics added).[19]

It's time for us to look at ourselves and take responsibility for the ways we've been apathetic, complicit, or worse in creating a need for marginalized groups to shock society out of its slumber. It's time to repent for "what we have done, and what we have left undone," as the confessional prayer goes. This requires, as the philosopher George Yancy has written, that "you look at parts of yourself that might cause pain and terror." Yancy modeled this kind of personal accountability by writing a *New York Times* op-ed copping to his own sexism and the way he had failed to stand up for women in the past.[20]

It's scary to look at our own racism, sexism, or bigotry. It's terrifying to contend with our own selfishness or indifference while people around us suffered in plain sight. It's painful to reckon with the ways we have mistreated people, often unknowingly. As *New York Times* columnist Charles Blow notes, a lack of understanding and empathy can cause grave harm to others, whether that's your intent or not.[21]

For some, it's mortifying to face the oppressive history of the country they love. Many Americans were raised on fairy tales about our heritage that whitewashed much of the brutality, oppression, and inequality out of the picture. The truth will set you free, but first it might break your heart. We need brokenhearted people overflowing with empathy if we want to heal this country.

Just remember, grace is not a "get-out-of-jail-free" card. It's not a weapon to be wielded to excuse or erase our failures. To believe either of these things is to make a grave category mistake. Rather than abusing the endless grace that so many of us have been shown, we should focus on pouring a portion of it back into the world as we labor toward the vision of a Beloved Community where there is such a love of our fellow citizens that we will accept nothing less than justice and equality for all.

Chapter 6

PEOPLE ARE NOT DISPOSABLE

How do we hold people accountable for wrongdoing and
yet at the same time remain in touch with their humanity enough to
believe in their capacity to be transformed?

—BELL HOOKS[1]

In 2020, a video from a Georgia prison went viral.[2] More than
20 million people were mesmerized by the scene of two inmates rushing to save a deputy who appeared to be in medical
distress. The incident was reported in news outlets around the
globe.

A few hours before midnight, Mitchell Smalls noticed Deputy Warren Hobbs slump and appear to pass out while sitting
at the desk from which he watched over the inmates. Smalls hit
the buzzer in his cell, and when Hobbs didn't respond, he
started frantically banging on the door. "I started going crazy
to wake everyone, banging . . . with all I had," Smalls told *The
Atlanta Journal-Constitution*.[3] "I was hoping the deputy wouldn't
fall from his chair, because it's high, but he fell. His head
slammed on the floor and there was so much blood."

The other inmates heard Smalls and joined in. "It was a sym-
phony of slamming fists and bodies against heavy, locked
doors; some men even lying on their backs to exert more force

with their legs, the thick glass windows in each door trembling in response," reported the Atlanta paper. The banging roused Hobbs long enough to make eye contact with two inmates in his line of vision. He hit the buzzer to open their door and the two men, Walter Whitehead and Terry Loveless, rushed to Hobbs and made the call for help that likely saved his life from the cardiac event that had caused him to lose consciousness.

One of the most "liked" comments on the video, with twenty-five thousand thumbs-ups, read, "There's a difference between bad decisions and bad people."[4]

This is one of the hallmarks of grace: to not see people as the sum total of their mistakes, bad decisions, or even bad beliefs. It's recognizing that others are multidimensional beings who can likely do better if given the chance. When we lose sight of these truths, we can be deluded into believing that cruel and inhumane punishments are the natural consequences of bad behavior.

It's telling that the term *cancel culture* is rarely used to describe the most canceled people in our country: those who have been swallowed whole by the criminal justice system. In many states, these individuals get tagged for the rest of their lives as "felons" and lose their right to participate in democracy through voting for various periods of time.[5] If they manage to escape a system designed to keep them on the hamster wheel of injustice, they will have to inform every employer in perpetuity of the crime for which they already paid their time. It's a system so utterly devoid of grace and rife with cruelty, vengeance, racism, and economic discrimination that it needs to be dismantled and built back up from scratch.

In a 2015 *New York Times* story about Norway's Halden Prison, considered the world's most humane maximum-security facility, journalist Jessica Benko aptly described the American approach to incarceration as "extravagant brutality." She described Halden as more than just a humane prison. It was, she wrote, "the physical expression of an entire national philosophy about the relative merits of punishment and forgiveness."[6]

In the same way, the "extravagant brutality" of our criminal justice system is a physical manifestation of America's philosophy of punishment and forgiveness. It's no accident that when people join an online mob against a person who has done something to deeply offend their sense of right and wrong, they can unconsciously mimic the graceless retribution that we mete out to people who break the law.

This doesn't mean that you can never use social media to seek accountability when someone is causing harm. Indeed, sometimes social media is the only recourse, as discussed in the previous chapter. It is often the only place where people who don't have a voice in the broader culture can express their views to a large audience and seek accountability. But a tool that can be used for justice and accountability can also be wielded as a weapon of domination and destruction.

When quests for accountability spin out of control, social media mobs act as judge, jury, and executioner. Anyone who pushes back on the adopted narrative runs the risk of having the mob turn on them. We see brutal shaming, vilification, and often successful attempts to ostracize the target, to get them fired and/or deplatformed. It often seems the goal is not just to cause them to lose their current employment or platform, but to make it impossible for them to find future opportunities. The entire event can often unfold with an aura of glee.

What sometimes is described as "accountability" in our online culture might be better described as "annihilation." We can delude ourselves into believing we are engaging in a dispassionate attempt to hold a person responsible for a wrong when we are behaving more like people in search of vengeance.

Revenge, because it's driven by rage and injury, is often not proportionate to the original offense. "Revenge doesn't say, 'An eye for an eye.' It says, 'You take my eye, and I'll blow out your brains,'" writes Yale theologian Miroslav Volf in his book *Free of Charge: Giving and Forgiving in a Culture Stripped of Grace*. "It doesn't say, 'An insult for an insult.' It says, 'You cross me once, you cross me twice, and I'll destroy your character and your career.' It doesn't say, 'You organize an act of terror, and we'll punish you.' It says, 'You organize an act of terror, and we'll use the overwhelming military force of a superpower to recast the political landscape of the entire region from which you came.' Revenge abandons the principle of 'measure for measure' and, acting out of injured pride and untamed fear, gives itself to punitive excess."[7]

We know we are seeing vengeance when the punishment doesn't fit the crime. As recounted in Jon Ronson's book *So You've Been Publicly Shamed,* Lindsey Stone posed in front of a sign at Arlington Cemetery that read SILENCE AND RESPECT while she flipped the bird and pretended to yell. She and a girl-friend often took stupid photographs, like of themselves smoking in front of a No Smoking sign. But somehow this picture made it from her personal Facebook page, which she thought was private, into the public domain. A "Fire Lindsey Stone" Facebook page garnered twelve thousand "likes," and her employer was inundated with emails demanding she be fired from her job at an independent living facility for adults with learning difficulties.[8]

Stone apologized but ultimately lost her job and couldn't find work for a year, during which time she went into a depression and barely left the house. Meanwhile, she was harassed online by people telling her that she "should be shot or exiled from the United States," and worse. When Ronson caught up with her eighteen months later, Stone told him, "Literally overnight, everything I knew and loved was gone."[9]

How was any of this proportionate to what occurred? Yet we often see people having their lives blown up over a single tweet, picture, or video. This is not the national crisis that some people have made it out to be, particularly the Extremely On-line conservatives, who have appropriated and weaponized the idea of "cancellation" as a way to demonize liberals and treat legitimate accountability as an affront to decent society. But that doesn't mean it's not a problem. Lindsey Stone, and people like her who become targets of online witch hunts, are not disposable.

It's worth noting that the Lindsey Stone mob was unleashed by conservatives, not so-called liberal snowflakes. It wasn't an isolated incident, either—conservatives "cancel" people all the time. Colin Kaepernick lost his NFL quarterback position doing the one thing he had dedicated his life to since childhood because conservatives couldn't tolerate him kneeling during the national anthem to protest police brutality.

USA Today editor Hemal Jhaveri lost her job in March 2021 following conservative outrage over a tweet she sent suggesting the assailant in a mass shooting would end up being a white man.[10] (It turned out he was of Middle Eastern descent.) She apologized and deleted the tweet, but she said in a blog post that *USA Today* chose to fire her after almost eight years with the company, an unfortunately completely predictable outcome in our current environment. The mob attack on her was vengeance personified. Journalist Lauren Wolfe lost her *New York Times* freelance editor gig in early 2021 after a libertarian journalist who is part of the anti–"cancel culture" brigade launched an online attack against her for tweeting that seeing President Joe Biden landing at Joint Base Andrews gave her chills.[11]

And this isn't a new phenomenon. Conservatives were canceling people for offending them back in 2003, when country music stations stopped playing the band the Chicks (then known as the Dixie Chicks) for criticizing George W. Bush.[12] Whoopi Goldberg has spoken out recently about how she was "canceled" by conservatives in 2004 for making a mildly raunchy joke about then President George W. Bush.[13] She lost engagements she had already booked and couldn't find work for many years. Goldberg said she had run through her savings and had no idea what she was going to do when Barbara Walters gave her a second chance by offering her a job as a cohost on *The View.* [14]

Online mobs have also been known to harm innocent people. Liberal Twitter went after a San Diego man, Emmanuel Cafferty, in June 2020 after a user posted a picture in which they claimed Cafferty was making a white supremacist hand signal (which looks like the "okay" sign) near a Black Lives Matter rally. Cafferty, who is Mexican American, says he was cracking his knuckles in the viral photo. In the end, Cafferty says he lost his job at San Diego Gas & Electric over this one unsubstantiated accusation after his employer received calls demanding his firing.[15] The local NBC news station reported that the man who posted the picture told them that he "may have gotten 'spun up' about the interaction and misinterpreted it [and] never intended for Cafferty to lose his job."

Even when the offense has definitely occurred and the cause is just, the tactics can sometimes be overly punitive, unforgiving, and disinterested in seeing gradations of harm. Such responses can look a lot like bullying. Also, not every incident requires a Category 5 hurricane of condemnation.

Sometimes a little grace might do the job.

At Smith College, Professor Loretta Ross teaches a course called White Supremacy in the Age of Trump and another called Reproductive Justice. She's concerned about "the speed in which the technology allows [disputes] to become viral, and quickly organizes a punishment squad of strangers."[16]

Professor Ross, who is the author of the forthcoming book *Calling In the Calling Out Culture,* echoed a concern I heard from other progressive activists "that most of our hostility is aimed horizontally at each other." This means a person can say or do a single thing that upsets their community and suddenly find themselves being publicly shamed and ultimately ostracized by their former community. "Liberal Twitter feels like a poorly designed videogame in which you never actually play against the other team," the progressive pastor Nadia Bolz-Weber told me. "All you do is get ranking points by pointing out how your own team members are wrong."[17] These purity spirals are self-defeating because they undermine cohesion and distract the group's energy from focusing on the problems that led to the formation of the community or group in the first place.

Ross teaches her students to "call in" rather than "call out." "If a person commits harm, whether it's in the current moment or in the past, if they're willing to acknowledge that they've committed harm and are willing to try and figure out . . . what they can do to remediate their harm and change their behavior so that they don't repeat the harm in the future, I want you to call them in, because we all make mistakes," Ross explained to me.[18] She learned about calling people in when she worked for the civil rights legend Rev. C. T. Vivian, a field general for Rev. Dr. Martin Luther King Jr. He always reminded Ross, "When you ask people to give up hate, you have to be there for them when they do."

What might "calling in" look like? Maybe before you tweet a screenshot with the demand that someone else "do better!" take a pause. How would you like to be treated if you messed up? Why not reach out to them and see if you can have a conversation? Consider giving them an opportunity to learn and apologize. If you are upset by something they wrote or tweeted a decade ago, approach the issue with some curiosity. Ask them if they still believe it, and if not, what do they believe now? Do they understand how harmful this belief is and are they willing to apologize? If your co-worker says or does something offensive, rather than unloading on them in front of other employees, consider pulling them aside for a private conversation.

If you don't have the energy to deal with someone who has said something or done something offensive—perhaps you are a woman who heard a sexist comment—maybe ask another person you trust to call the person in.

To be clear, sending someone a direct message saying, "That post you just put up is misogynist and you obviously hate women. Take it down now," isn't "calling in" just because you are doing it privately. That's an attack, not a conversation starter. Try something like "Today's post plays on sexist stereotypes and it's really demeaning to women. I think you should apologize and take the post down." If you have the emotional bandwidth and time, you could offer to discuss it further on the phone or through email or direct message.

Calling in is an act of grace. It's a type of accountability that is oriented toward helping people change and making our society more just and equal. It's fundamentally restorative, not retributive. It recognizes the inherent dignity in every person and doesn't treat others as if they are disposable if they say or do the wrong thing.

Using the tactic of calling in actually happens more than people realize. As the previous chapter demonstrates, people who are characterized as being "canceled" often had been given earlier opportunities to change their behavior or apologize before the issue became public, and chose not to. They had been called in but didn't listen. I've called in various people over the years, and the ones who waved me off and continued their behavior ultimately became aggrieved when they were held publicly accountable down the line. I have a friend who was called in by an antiracist leader who could have blasted him online and instead told him directly that some of his behavior was problematic. My friend listened, offered a public apology, and started to do the work to change how he interacted online.

A time that I was called in really stands out in my mind, even though it was fifteen years ago. I briefly had a blog, and one day

I posted about a group of Black women in Atlanta who had organized a protest against misogynist lyrics in rap music. Essentially, I agreed with their position, and knowing me back then, I probably went on some antimisogyny rant. Almost immediately my phone rang and my friend, a Black woman, told me, "You need to take that post down now."

I was totally perplexed. I was agreeing with the Black women, so what was wrong? She told me that it wasn't the substance of what I wrote that was the problem. The issue was that while I thought I was standing in solidarity with my fellow women, it would be experienced by many African Americans as a white woman critiquing Black culture. If I kept the post up, people might be offended.

At the time, I saw the world through a white feminist paradigm that was not intersectional. I saw women who opposed misogynist lyrics on one side and men who supported them on the other side. I had no understanding of how adding race to the mix changed the dynamics. Nonetheless, I knew enough to recognize that if one of my Black friends took the time to pick up the phone to call me to complain about something I wrote, I needed to listen. I deleted the post, and when I later mentioned it to another Black friend, he affirmed that what I wrote was not okay and taking it down was the right thing to do. Who knows how many people I might have offended and disrespected if my friend hadn't taken the time to call me in?

If you are at a point where calling in isn't an option or you have tried that and you feel you need to call someone out online, ask yourself a few questions: Are you reluctantly doing this because you want to see a type of harmful behavior end and can't just ignore it? Or are you doing it gleefully, and if you're honest, you're kind of loving the idea of seeing this person "get what they deserve"? Is the person actually causing harm, or did they just offend you by expressing a view you don't share? Are you aware that your attempt at accountability has a decent chance of snowballing and ending with this person's life in tatters? Is it possible you don't have the full story?

I often see activist leaders call people out for problematic behavior in a reasonable and respectful manner. Then their followers pick up the ball and run with it to places well beyond what that leader expressed. This is frequently where I notice the most viciousness and bullying. A swarm gathers, starts to gain momentum and takes on a life of its own. The person who has caused the offense ceases to be seen as a human being and serves more as a virtual punching bag. The nasty attacks being hurled at them can't possibly be expected to help them see the light or change. By now, people should have noticed that shaming others typically causes them to double down out of self-preservation.

We need to bear in mind that it's almost impossible to offer a proportionate response over the Internet. While each individual may feel that they are just calling for accountability, the combined effect of thousands of people attacking one person inflicts a kind of psychological devastation on the target that I don't think we really appreciate, especially if five minutes ago they were not a public figure. Contacting someone's employer to get them fired really should be the option of last resort in cases where serious harm has occurred.

It's also important to remember that the most problematic cases of so-called cancel culture could not have occurred were it not for the soulless nature of employment in the United States, where many employers see the people who work for them as mostly disposable. In this environment, they will throw an employee overboard at the first hint of trouble to avoid a public relations nightmare.

As *Atlantic* writer Helen Lewis has pointed out, "Brands will gravitate toward low-cost, high-noise signals as a substitute for genuine reform, to ensure their survival."[19] Firing someone for a single mistake to appease a Twitter mob costs a self-interested employer nothing. It would be much more challenging for them to behave like they have a responsibility to their employee. They could provide the employee the counseling or training they need, have them make apologies and amends as necessary, and allow them to be a part of transforming the culture at the workplace.

I often see people making light of someone being publicly shamed and losing their job and reputation. "Oh, they'll be fine," people will say. But how on earth could anyone know this? For most people in America, losing employment means losing not just your income, but also your health insurance. They may be supporting a child or a spouse with a chronic illness. They may be caring for elderly parents. Because they've been publicly attacked, their misdeed lives on in perpetuity on the Internet, which can make getting new employment difficult while leaving them burdened with debilitating shame. Sometimes firing a person may be the only option and an appropriate punishment, but we need to be honest about the ramifications of a public shaming that leads to job and reputational loss.

The British scholar Mary Beard, like so many women in the public eye, is the recipient of a near-constant stream of misogynist emails and online comments. When the author of *Women & Power: A Manifesto* retweeted a misogynist attack from a university student that is too vile to repeat here, the student posted an apology and Beard accepted his invitation to lunch. They have stayed in touch, and Beard has provided letters of reference for the repentant harasser. "He is going to find it hard to get a job, because as soon as you Google his name that is what comes up," she told *The New Yorker*. "And although he was a very silly, injudicious, and at that moment not very pleasant young guy, I don't actually think one tweet should ruin your job prospects."[20]

Beard demonstrated grace by recognizing the concept of proportionality and rejecting the "all or nothing" way we often see people who do or say offensive and harmful things.

It's a reminder to deal with someone who commits a first offense differently than we would a repeat offender. A person who quickly and sincerely apologizes and pledges to do better doesn't deserve the same treatment as someone who has engaged in the same problematic or harmful behavior repeatedly, has refused to change, and won't apologize until their job hangs in the balance. We need to be able to recognize the difference between a person who messed up but wants to do better and a person who has no interest in learning or changing their behavior. Moreover, offenses that happened recently shouldn't be treated the same way as those in the distant past. People change, and getting someone fired for something that happened in their past for which they are sorry, and in which they no longer believe, often feels vengeful.

Different levels of harm require different responses. Sometimes offering grace means just accepting a sincere apology and moving on. In other instances it means demanding accountability and creating space for the person who caused the harm to engage in the multilayered process of repentance and repair. Depending on the harm caused, this process could take minutes or it could take years.

A baseline rule—which should sound familiar even to non-Christians—is that we should do unto others as we'd have done unto us. If every person on Twitter stopped and just asked these simple questions—When I've screwed up, how did I want people to approach me? Is what I'm about to say how I would want someone to talk to me?—Twitter would become exponentially less toxic. The same questions should be asked when we look at our criminal justice system. If we committed a crime, would we want to be locked up in a tiny room and be all but forgotten? Would we want to be treated as nothing more than the sum of our worst behavior, or would we want the opportunity to learn from our mistake, bring wholeness where we caused harm, and return to society as a better person?

When we see disproportionate punishment or online mobs

demanding complete destruction of other people for real or perceived offenses, it can be because they are acting in vengeance. But it also can be that they're engaging in the "scapegoat mechanism"—a term coined by the French philosopher René Girard—that's as old as humanity. This unconscious impulse drives us to heap the culture's sins onto one person, or one group of people. Scapegoating "bad" people is an electrifying experience, and none of us are immune to it. "Hatred holds a group together much more quickly and easily than love and inclusivity," Richard Rohr says.[21]

In the Bible, a scapegoat is an animal designated to bear the burdens of a society's collective sins through a ritual, then driven into the wilderness. This is in effect what our society does when we designate certain people or groups of people to carry the weight of all our sins. The destruction of the scapegoat creates a shared sense that a meaningful purging has taken place.

Scapegoats in their truest form are completely innocent. In American history, most immigrants have been scapegoated upon arriving in America. They are blamed for anything that goes wrong, even though the problems are not caused by them. In Germany, Hitler scapegoated Jews, blaming them for the economic and social problems Germany faced and for which they were not responsible. Long ago, people who were accused of being "witches" were executed following ill-fated events (a bad harvest or the death of a child or even cattle) over which they obviously had no control.[22] Black people have been the most consistently scapegoated group of people in the United States, and this treatment continues to this day.

Our prisons are filled with Black people who were scapegoated for rising drug use in the 1970s and increased crime in the 1980s and early 1990s. Throughout our history, Black men have been scapegoated for crimes committed by white people, losing their freedom and often their lives as a result. They have been arrested or killed because of false accusations against them by white women. This isn't just some faraway problem; it still happens today, which is why there was such an overwhelming outcry when Amy Cooper, a white woman walking her dog, lied to police about Christian Cooper, a black birder, threatening her safety in Central Park.[23]

But a scapegoat doesn't have to be completely innocent. It can be a person who has done something wrong but experiences a disproportionate backlash or punishment because members of society are heaping all their rage, anxiety, and fury about systemic problems on this one person. For example, Boeing's head of communications was forced to resign in 2020 after an employee complained about an article he'd written thirty-three years prior, at the age of twenty-nine, arguing that women shouldn't be permitted to fight in combat.[24] It may well be that the employee who complained was someone who had experienced discrimination in her career and now had a chance to hold someone accountable. God knows I've been there. But I would argue that it's not fair for a person to lose their job over an article written three decades ago with which they no longer agree—and which unfortunately reflected the common view of society at the time.

No one person should be forced to bear the sins of society's terrible behavior. They should be held responsible for what they did, not for what other people did. In the case of the Boeing executive, this might have been an opportunity for Boeing to ask him to head up an effort to help attract more female pilots or to create a program that supported the development of women in the organization. There are ways to address past wrongs that create the opportunity for healing and don't involve getting someone fired.

People often say in the wake of the latest so-called cancel culture controversy that we have lost our capacity to forgive or to believe that people can change. I wonder if we ever really had it. It seems to me that if forgiveness was a central value in our culture, our criminal justice system wouldn't look like it does. But it's certainly a capacity we need to develop if we want our culture to be less brutal.

In early-2021, journalist Alexi McCammond resigned as editor in chief of *Teen Vogue* two weeks after she was appointed to the position.[25] Her decision came in the wake of a staff revolt regarding anti-Asian and homophobic tweets she'd sent a decade earlier, when she was seventeen. She had apologized for the tweets in 2019, and though she offered a fulsome apology in response to the new backlash, it didn't help her.

Many people took to social media to complain that "cancel culture" had struck again, this time harming a Black woman no less. The situation was more complicated than that, but what struck me was how so many portrayed McCammond's teenage views as ineradicably woven into her being. It made my heart ache for all of us—this is the "all or nothing" framework that rules so many of our psyches.

But if this were true, we would all be screwed.

If a person can't change over a ten-year period—between being a teenager and becoming a full-grown adult—then what hope is there for us? Of course I view this all through my own experience, where I look at the person I was even five years ago and find her unrecognizable. The fact is, most people change throughout life. Indeed, it turned out a *Teen Vogue* staffer who opposed McCammond's hiring had used the N-word in multiple tweets a little over a decade ago; she was Latina and was tweeting to a white friend. (Sometimes we also have an unconscious need to scapegoat others for things we ourselves have done or even failed to do.) I imagine she is a different person today than she was when she made those tweets, unless there are similar tweets or comments made recently. McCammond ultimately may have not been a good fit for the job, but the public shaming she experienced for tweets made as a teenager for which she was sorry was hard to watch. There but for the grace of God go most of us.

It seems that allowing a portion of grace into our world might temper the graceless and overly simplistic "do the crime, do the time" mentality with which many of us have been indoctrinated. It might pull us out of the divisive "us vs. them" paradigm and help us start seeing each other with empathy and as multidimensional human beings who are not disposable.

We have to choose to be different kinds of people if we want to have a different kind of country. Demonization, domination, and dehumanization got us into this mess.

Grace just might help lead us out of it.

Chapter 7

THROUGH A GLASS DARKLY

We don't see things as they are, we see things as we are.

—Anaïs Nin[1]

*I*f there is one practical idea that encapsulates grace, it's the belief that people are doing the best they can with what they have.

People who believe this are more likely to cut others slack, give them the benefit of the doubt, and remember they don't know what's going on in a person's life or what traumas or wounds have shaped them. The saying "Be kind, for everyone you meet is fighting a hard battle" is their guiding principle. People who think this way don't label others as inherently "bad" or "good." They don't feel the need to demonize the "other side." They can hold others accountable with humanity.

In other words: they know how to practice grace.

When I first read Brené Brown's claim that people are usually doing the best they can,[2] my immediate reaction was "No, Brené, they aren't." In my judgy little head, I ticked off all the people who I knew were not trying hard enough. I had just learned about how dualism was clouding my vision and was straining to wrap my brain around a new way of thinking, but I felt enormous resistance to applying this idea to people whom I didn't like or who were angering me. It was one thing to say that about a friend or a like-minded person, or even a family member with whom I had strong disagreements. It was an entirely different feat to offer this grace to the people who were driving me to the brink of madness.

As I learned more about myself and the roots of my struggle with grace, I came to realize that some people find it much easier to adopt this viewpoint than others. When we are grounded and emotionally integrated, the world looks one way. When we are saddled with unprocessed trauma or wounds, the world takes on an entirely different hue.

"Trauma" has become a zeitgeisty buzzword that may engender eye rolls from people who feel this concept has been abused and overused to the point the word is rendered nearly meaningless. If you are allergic to the word *trauma,* just think of it as "that incredibly painful thing that happened to me that I still haven't processed and healed from." It's important to understand how we are affected by deeply painful experiences when we fail to integrate them.

Through the lens of a person who has had their trauma activated, the world looks utterly black and white. Unprocessed trauma can turbocharge a dualistic propensity and push it into a particularly destructive zone. In the traumatized person's binary framework, you are either with them or against them. It doesn't matter if you are doing the best you can, because a person who has had their trauma activated by another person has little capacity to harbor empathy for that individual. They need to direct what energy they have toward keeping themselves feeling safe. Even if they thought to stop and consider that the person who has activated them probably has more going on than meets the eye—if they tried to see the total humanity or the divine spark within this person—their nervous system is too jacked up to view any situation clearly. This is a physiological process that is completely unconscious and cannot be overridden by reason.

"Trauma creates shame. When there's shame, there's no grace for self, and if there is no grace for self, there is no grace for others," Courtney Leak, a trauma-informed therapist, explained in an interview. "Grace requires an emotional and psychological capacity that trauma takes away from us."[3]

What many of us don't realize is how much our behavior is unconsciously driven by our autonomic nervous system, which is very sensitive. "When it detects threat, it activates a series of responses, and this cascade of neurotransmitters and hormones go off inside of our body to prepare us to fight or flight," clinical psychologist Christine Runyan noted in a 2021 interview.[4] Most of us have heard of this phenomenon, but few of us really appreciate how much our behavior and the behavior of others is driven by these completely unconscious physiological factors.

This process was a survival mechanism that helped early humans react to occasional life-threatening events, like being chased by a tiger. But for the person with unprocessed trauma, the same response can be activated by non-life-threatening events, such as another person posting something offensive on Facebook or a family member discussing their support for a political candidate with offensive views. Because of the massive amounts of information we take in (thanks to the power of the Internet and 24/7 news cycles), this process can put our systems in a constant state of arousal. Our bodies were not built to be burdened with this level of chronic stress.

"Our bodies exist in the present. To your thinking brain, there is past, present and future, but to a traumatized body there is only now. That now is the home of intense survival strategy," writes trauma therapist Resmaa Menakem.[5]

This is why it's important that we learn to pay attention to what is happening in our bodies. When you feel activated, and the fury or panic starts rising, it's not the ideal time to post on social media or react to a family member. Instead, Leak suggests you ask yourself some questions: "Have I eaten today? Do I feel safe in my body? Have I run this past a trusted friend?"[6]

She suggests you sit in silence and consider if the issue that has activated you is historical. When we're hysterical, it's usually historical, Leak reminds us. Hysterical doesn't have to mean that we are screaming like a banshee. It just means that we should touch base with ourselves to notice if we are emotionally activated and if so, take a minute to do an inventory of why that might be, and get our bodies and minds settled down before we move ahead with conversations or social media posts. We should also ask ourselves if we are potentially engaging in scapegoating. In other words, is our rage proportionate to what this person did or does it grow out of cumulated fury that has not been processed or expressed in a more productive manner that doesn't involve heaping the sins of society onto one human being?

All of our bodies are designed to have physiological reactions to threats. But a person with unhealed trauma has a much narrower window of tolerance and their nervous system can be activated by lower levels of threat.[7] So what is just a disagreement to one person can feel like an emotional assault to another.

A person who has gone into "fight" mode may become aggressive and refuse to back down. If "flight" is the response, that person may emotionally or physically remove themselves from the conflict or threatening situation. In addition to these two responses, there is a "freeze" response, which is activated by the parasympathetic nervous system. People who experience this might become overly passive and shut down in the face of a threat, mistreatment, or injustice. It might feel unsafe to them to fight or flee. People engaging in "flight" or "freeze" may at times appear to be responding with grace; they look like they are being patient or tolerant of other people's upsetting behavior when they are actually having a trauma response and their body is on high alert.

It doesn't occur to most people that they may have unresolved trauma or that the people around them are in the same boat. We tend to associate the word *trauma* with unambiguous brutality: physical abuse, sexual assault, kidnapping, being witness to a murder, or being abandoned as a child. But trauma can also involve things that aren't made-for-Hollywood horrific. Having a narcissistic parent or spouse can cause emotional trauma. Growing up in a controlling religious environment can create trauma. Moving constantly as a child or being shamed for having a body shape that doesn't conform to toxic cultural standards can constitute trauma. There is also vicarious trauma. Sometimes it's hearing about something that happened to another person or watching a terrifying event—think the 9/11 attacks or George Floyd being tortured to death—that can create individual and societal trauma.[8]

Trauma experienced by members of oppressed racial groups is horrific and always humming below the surface, where it's not obvious to the dominant racial group. "Although similar to posttraumatic stress disorder, racial trauma is unique in that it involves ongoing individual and collective injuries due to exposure and reexposure to race-based stress," a 2019 study published in the *American Psychologist* noted.[9] The insistence of so many white people that the racism doesn't exist means that other racial groups are constantly being gaslit, which can be extremely traumatic.

It's important to note that trauma is not event specific; it is person specific. How we respond to events depends on nature, nurture, and a host of other factors. A parents' divorce can be a trauma (as it was for me) if the child is unable to process their emotions about it. But if the child is able to work through their pain or fear with their parents or a trusted adult, then it may resolve itself as merely a bad memory—or even one with a happy ending, about how a family navigated a difficult situation with compassion and love—instead of a trauma that haunts them through adulthood. That said, there are some events that are inherently traumatic and it's unimaginable anyone could walk away unscathed. No amount of nature or nurture will make being sexually assaulted or molested not a traumatic event, for example.

Then there are wounds that may not merit the "trauma" label but have still shaped us deeply. It's possible we feel embarrassed about raising them, given that they seem so minor or happened so long ago. Why would anybody want to hear about the time a boy at the roller rink told my friend he didn't want to skate with twelve-year-old me because I was ugly? Why share with anyone the time my seventh-grade best friend dumped me to hang out with another, "cooler" girl?

I'll tell you why. When I write those sentences, I can still feel the memories coursing through my body like ground glass. Our lives are filled with events that might seem ludicrously trivial but that, if we neglect to process and integrate them, live on as we unconsciously work them out at the expense of others—and ourselves, for that matter.

As we do our own work, we should seek to have empathy for those who have not yet realized what they are carrying around and working out on other people. Recognizing that people have unhealed traumas or wounds, or may currently be struggling through a traumatic event, depression, or some other hardship, does not mean that we are required to be their punching bags. It just means that rather than reacting to someone else's hurtful or harmful behavior with judgment or reciprocal nastiness, we could try offering a little grace. When we consider that people are doing the best they can with the tools they have, it can completely reframe challenging situations.

When I was deep into writing this book, one day I had an "aha moment" regarding my mother, with whom I'd always had a tumultuous relationship. I had harbored so much resentment and anger for so long, and no amount of therapy could rid me of it. But in that moment, as I thought of my twenty-something mother facing an unplanned pregnancy while pursuing her Ph.D., my body was flooded with empathy. I thought of how she was forced into a more conventional life than she wanted by the expectations of society and her Catholic parents. By the time she figured out she was living someone else's life, she had two children and a husband.

She was also dealing with Olympian levels of stress as she worked as a trailblazer leading the way for future women. She was perpetually battling the discrimination and sexual harassment she and her female students experienced in an unapologetically male-dominated environment. It must have been exhausting. I could see it so clearly now: *she was doing the best she could with what she had.* No parent has a child with the intention of hurting or disappointing them; parents want their children to be happy. My mother was no different.

Sometimes, recognizing that someone is doing the best they can might mean ignoring them when they act out, or it can mean responding to them respectfully even if they refused to offer you or others the same courtesy. The comedian Sarah Silverman did this in 2018 when a man sent her a nasty and misogynist tweet. By checking his Twitter time line, she saw he had suffered many struggles and setbacks. So rather than giving him the snarky smackdown that would have thrilled the Twitter crowd, she replied instead by saying, "I believe in you . . . I see what ur doing & your rage is thinly veiled pain . . . I know this feeling . . . see what happens when u choose love. I see it in you."[10]

He responded by pouring out his heart about his problems. Silverman offered him encouragement and empathy. She suggested he find a support group for his emotional distress and urged him to see a doctor about back pain that was plaguing him. She put a call out to her followers to offer him support,

which they did. He ended up apologizing to her, found a doctor, and raised money through a GoFundMe campaign to help
cover his medical costs.

A week after his first message to Silverman, he tweeted,
"Thank you to all the support financially, emotionally, and do-
nations. This is more than I could have wished for . . . Thank u
everyone. U showed me a lot within a few days. Love u all."

That's the power of grace.

Hurt people hurt people, the cliché goes. It's also true that
healed people can help heal others, their communities, and
even their country. Which is why everyone should take a look
at their own emotional history and consider whose trauma or
wounds they may be bumping up against when they find themselves in toxic conflicts with family members, friends, and co-
workers, or constantly activated by what they see on social
media or in the news.

One simple way to determine if you experienced childhood
trauma is to take the Adverse Childhood Experiences or ACE
test, which is available online.[11] The test is based on a study the
Centers for Disease Control and Prevention calls "one of the
largest investigations of childhood abuse and neglect and house-
hold challenges and later-life health and well-being."[12]

According to the Centers for Disease Control and Prevention, an adverse childhood experience is a potentially traumatic
event that occurs before the age of eighteen. Roughly 61 percent of adults surveyed said they had experienced at least one
type of ACE, and nearly 1 in 6 had experienced four or more
types of ACEs.[13] It's important to note that the test is not all-
inclusive; for example, it doesn't account for traumatic experiences such as racism and other forms of discrimination or
deaths in the family. It also doesn't account for traumatic events
you may have experienced as an adult.

Out of curiosity, one day I took the ACE test and was
shocked by my score: I had experienced six of the ten potentially traumatic childhood experiences listed. I then began to

take stock of how the emotional turmoil in my career was intertwined with my unexamined trauma—from both my childhood and a succession of scarifying personal losses in my midthirties. Those tragic events activated ever deeper needs for psychological safety and certainty, which in turn led me to seek emotional refuge in ways that only worsened things.

The first and most brutal blow came without the slightest warning, laying waste to my cozy life in the West Village apartment I shared with my new puppy, Ellie. Near the end of 2003, I was blindsided by a phone call from my stepmother, Alicia. "I'm sorry to have to tell you this, Kirsten, but your father died today." He was only sixty-one. It had happened quickly—a massive heart attack took my brilliant, complicated, and tender-hearted father down instantly—so there had been no time for goodbyes.

Looking back, I can see that deep and unaddressed childhood trauma had loaded up inside of me like a stick of dynamite, with my father's death lighting the fuse. Losing a parent, especially prematurely and unexpectedly, is always painful. But what I experienced was on another level and can only be explained by what mental health experts call "cumulative trauma burden." I stopped eating, dropping fifteen pounds off my already lean body in just a month. I continued to shed weight until I was carrying a mere 120 pounds on my five-foot-eight frame.

I had managed an anxiety disorder with an antidepressant since my twenties, but my medication was no match for this new form of agony. Switching to a different antidepressant only seemed to make things worse. In addition to suffering from paralyzing anxiety and depression, I became suicidal, nearly ending my life on one occasion. Every day became a struggle to just stay alive. I switched medications again and the suicidal ideation subsided, but the depression and anxiety remained my constant companions.

Barely a year later—as I was slowly finding my footing—my sweet, selfless, unintentionally hilarious grandmother died. She was the most important person in my life; we had been deeply intertwined since my childhood, and life without her was unimaginable. The bad news just kept coming: the year she passed, my bursting-with-life stepfather was diagnosed with terminal liver cancer.

In addition to the continued shrinking of my already small family, my work life was becoming increasingly stressful. I had begun doing television on a regular basis and ended up signing on as a contributor at Fox News. At the time, Fox was recognized as conservatives' answer to the mainstream media, but it hadn't yet become the bête noire of Democrats. Still, I wasn't used to the criticism that comes with being in the public eye. As I naïvely wandered into the world of cameras and microphones, I was bringing with me a furious tangle of unresolved and unacknowledged anguish.

As a wise friend of mine once observed of people in the public eye, "The world does not move forward on the shoulders of emotionally healthy people." Indeed, I would find myself clashing—on the air and in writing—with an army of other people who had their own binary worldviews, many of whom doubtless had their own unresolved or unexamined issues.

Even though my work was all-consuming, I felt utterly lost and untethered to anything that mattered. It was in this state that I was invited by a new boyfriend to attend church with him. I was less than enthused. As a child, I absorbed a fragile Christian faith from my father, but by sophomore year in college I was an atheist. I had developed disdain for all religion, Christianity most of all. I saw it as a bunch of silly hocus-pocus; the opiate of the masses, as Karl Marx famously characterized it. Also, this was New York City: Sundays were for brunch, not church.

Then a question popped into my head: *What if it's all true, and you didn't even try?* My world had been completely leveled, and I was desperate for something, anything, to make me feel whole again.

So it was that I found myself tagging along to a church service on the Upper East Side of Manhattan. I learned later that I'd been brought to a "seeker" church, which meant many of the people attending were either lapsed believers considering a path back to faith or nonbelievers who were curious about Christianity. All the preaching was oriented toward people who doubted, or flat-out rejected, the claims of Christianity. People like me, in other words. On that first Sunday, the pastor's talk turned out to be philosophical and intellectually stimulating. I was intrigued enough to give it another try—then another, and another, until I started being the one who made sure we got to the subway to make it to the service on time.

By 2006, the boyfriend and I were no more, but I had gone all in on Christianity, and not in a good way. Evangelical theology would prove combustible when mixed with my childhood trauma and recent losses. The absolute last thing I needed in my life was a framework that pushed me deeper into dualistic thinking where there was almost always a "right" way and a "wrong" way to do things. The Bible became a kind of oracle for me to consult so that I could be extra sure I was doing things the "right" way, which over time just left me feeling like I was coming up short, in turn spurring me to look for ways to be a better Christian.

Around this time, my stepfather, Bill, got up from the dinner table one evening, saying he was feeling tired. He went into the bedroom, lay down, and went into a coma. I flew home from New York to Alaska immediately. Bill lay unconscious in his bed, a crackling, wet sound accompanying each of his labored breaths. He passed away at home a few days later as I made chili in the kitchen. I knew he was gone because I could hear the hysterical wails of my mother from the bedroom.

Throughout all of this, I'm not sure there was even one person who knew how deeply I was suffering. In June 2018, in a *USA Today* column about the deaths of Kate Spade and Anthony Bourdain, I shared about my suicidal ideation following my father's death. The people who had been with me the most during that period were shocked. If those who saw me every day at work or my closest friends and family hadn't seen it, certainly people who viewed me on television or read my columns had no inkling of how unbearable my life was. They had no idea how unresolved trauma was jamming up my system. I didn't even know it myself.

It's a reminder that you really don't know what is going on in people's lives, and that you will never go wrong approaching a situation with a portion of grace. One week I was so desperate to die that I stuck my head in my oven, only to pull it out as images of my two younger brothers flashed before my eyes. The next week I was being interviewed for a profile by *Elle* magazine and named a "Power Punk" in the *New York Observer* for my work in politics. I'm sure to the outside world it looked like I had the perfect life. I can't tell you how many times during what would end up being the decade from Hell, I had people tell me "I saw you on TV and you looked so happy!" It understandably never occurred to anyone that I consciously took every ounce of energy I had and focused it on doing the best job I could when I was on air. What was I going to do—sit there and frown or start crying? That was for later, when I was alone in my apartment.

I wish I could say that my life got better, but it didn't. In 2008 I entered a relationship that led to marriage and then divorce, with more trauma added to the scale. The way the evangelical church I attended reacted to the situation not only did not alleviate my suffering, it actually made things worse. As I struggled to keep my head above water, one (former) friend invited me to coffee, only to pull out her Bible and point to the verse that said, "God hates divorce." Multiple pastors told me I should not get divorced, even after acknowledging how soul crushing my situation was, because my husband and I had not experienced the very narrow circumstances in which they believed the Bible allowed divorce. I was so traumatized and disempowered that I stayed, because I thought that's what a "good Christian" did.

Fortunately, my then-husband made the decision to leave, and we were divorced by the end of 2012. I had been struggling with fatigue and body pain since my father's death but had been able to mostly manage it. During my marriage, however, it tipped over into full-blown chronic fatigue syndrome. My symptoms were diagnosed by various doctors as chronic Lyme disease, Epstein-Barr virus, and fibromyalgia. I was in constant, crushing pain, slept fourteen hours at a time, and was still perpetually exhausted. It took me years to recover from the marriage and divorce, and perhaps just as important, from the emotional battering I had experienced throughout my time in the evangelical church, which I eventually left in 2015.

Sometimes I try to explain this period of my life this way: It's like I was driving down a road going in the right direction and a sudden detour forced me down another road. I drove and drove and drove and eventually found the original road again and turned back onto it. It sounds innocuous, until you realize I was on the wrong road for more than a decade. It's great when you get going back in the right direction. Contending with everything that happened during that detour period is another matter. At times, I've felt like I lost a decade of my life, unconscious and unaware of how distorted my view of the world could become in certain circumstances. That's what unprocessed trauma does to you, and probably to more people than you realize.

It wasn't until the end of 2018 that I found a therapist who could help me. She was "trauma informed," something I didn't even know existed until I was sitting in her office.

She explained that people develop different behavioral patterns in response to trauma, and that the one most dominant for me was called "the rigid strategy," which is common for people who engage in the "fight" response. It's the hyperbinary approach I fell back on when under stress. When people who use the rigid strategy are activated, it is hard for them to feel safe if they can't get people to see things their way. They react with hypervigilance, which can result in bullying people into agreeing with them and when they don't, shaming them in a last-ditch effort to force their compliance. If all of that fails, they toss those they're in conflict with into the "bad people" basket and heap condemnation upon them.

If you have spent five minutes on Twitter, you've seen the rigid strategy.

I learned also that I used dissociation, which is a common "flight" response, as a survival strategy. This meant I would mentally remove myself from whatever felt threatening at the time and retreat into myself. That's what I often did during my first few sessions, as my therapist and I began the process of excavating deeply buried traumas.

Growing up, I was basically an alien creature in my family. I was sensitive and deep and, according to my family, too emotional. My parents never cried. Their parents never cried. We were Irish; if you wanted to show an emotion, yelling was how it was done. All the better if it took the form of a blindsiding outburst over some minor incident. Then you'd quickly move on and go catch a movie together.

But I cried all the time. Not about typical kid things like my brother stealing my toy. I cried because I needed so much from my parents and they simply could not give it to me. I cried because there was so much suffering in the world. I cried because I wanted to process all my feelings, not just go see a movie after a fight. I cried because everyone in my family thought I was crazy for being so emotional. I cried and cried and cried until one day I didn't. Then emotional numbness and dissociation became my way of coping with the constant overwhelm of life. Coldly analyzing and reasoning my way through issues became my compulsion, and then interestingly, it became my actual job: political analyst.

Throughout my life, people had criticized me for daydreaming and being unaware of what was happening around me, and now I understood why. I had often heard about how aloof or cold or distant I could seem. It always shocked me, because I think most people who really know me view me as a deeply sensitive and caring person. But often my outside didn't match my insides. This bifurcated way of existing had benefited me professionally because it had allowed me to keep an emotional distance and calm in the face of other people's out-of-control or over-the-top behavior. At the same time, it had given me too high a tolerance for toxic relationships and environments. What I used to think of as "grace" was often just a trauma response.

Whatever our tendencies, we each just need to be aware that we might have unconscious strategies that will make it hard for us to practice grace with other people. If my reaction to disagreement when I'm stressed and tired is to engage in rigid thinking and fight back hard, where is the room for me to see other people in their full humanity? How can I create space for another person's way of thinking or being if my unconscious response is to engage in "flight" by dissociating and emotionally shutting down when I feel emotionally unsafe?

While I was gaining an intellectual understanding of the way trauma had shaped me, I was still struggling with the goal of abandoning altogether my binary thinking. In the meantime, my physical symptoms—which I had come to believe were psychosomatic responses to trauma—were improving only marginally. In mid-2019, I decided to attend an intensive one-week group therapy program at a place called Onsite in Tennessee, having been told by many friends that it had changed their lives.

While I was there, I worked through the trauma and unprocessed grief around the deaths of my father and grandmother. Three weeks after I returned home, I noticed that all of my fatigue and pain were gone. I felt happy and light. My capacity for understanding grace began to expand. That was two years ago, and the pain and fatigue have never returned for any extended period of time. But I do have flare-ups now and then. When this happens, I've learned to listen to my body, because it's telling me something needs to be processed or that I've overwhelmed my system. Often, I'm pushing myself too hard or holding myself to impossible standards.

In other words, I'm not giving myself grace.

I never really understood why Onsite had been such a physically and emotionally healing experience for me until I was interviewing Courtney Leak for this book. "Trauma can only be healed if we have been seen in it," she explained. "We freeze until we are seen in that place."[14]

Because the Onsite therapy was done in a group of ten people plus a therapist, my grief and trauma were witnessed and processed with people who could hold space for it objectively because they were not tied to it in any way. This is how you integrate trauma. As Leak explained, our families often can't hold that space for us because they are in so much pain themselves around whatever difficult event has occurred. This is why the difference between a trauma and a bad memory can be that the latter was witnessed and processed at the time it occurred.

"When trauma is integrated, a person's nervous system is no longer on high alert, or activated by things that used to trigger them," explains Austin Houghtaling, a therapist and vice president of Clinical Services at Onsite. "They can tell their story and stay present without dissociating. They can feel, without shutting down. They can stay 'in their body' and in the moment, and in their emotions without disconnecting from self or others."[15]

I also learned simple ways to discharge energy when I felt

overwhelmed—doing things that I used to think were bizarre and goofy but now view as essential tools to keep me grounded. In one Zoom session with my therapist, I was feeling anxious and angry about something in the news. She told me I could only express what I felt by using my body. I could not use words, but I could make other noises or hit something like my bed or chair. Poor Robert thought I was being murdered because I went from low-decibel groaning to screaming at the top of my lungs within seconds. My therapist then directed me to soothe my body by swinging my arms back and forth. By the time I was done, my anxiety was gone and I felt grounded and reset.

These are called somatic—meaning "of the body"—practices. There are many other forms that include humming or gently rocking. For me, crying is a somatic release, though before I went to Onsite I rarely cried as an adult. I was too disconnected from myself to get in touch with my own emotions. But for the entire week I was there, I cried almost nonstop, either while sharing my grief or witnessing other people process their own traumatizing experiences.

Later, at my therapist's suggestion, I bought a foam bat and now, when I feel that old pain, fatigue, or anxiety return, I grab it and whale on a big pillow. That poor pillow often gets an earful about whatever has upset me. Yes, I know this sounds super wacky, but I can't argue with the results. Sometimes I have to do this over multiple days, but ultimately it will reset my body. For minor frustrations, I just grab a pillow and scream into it. This is met with curious and concerned looks from my dogs, but rids me of the anxiety building in my body. Other times I shake my arms and legs to move the energy. I always follow with soothing myself to calm my system down after discharging the energy. For me, these practices have been life changing.

Once therapy had helped me to integrate past experiences

that had been traumatic, and I learned to be more tuned in to my body, I had a greater capacity for nuance and was able to give up my hypervigilant quest to protect myself from the "bad" people and their "bad" ideas. When I saw other people reacting in what seemed like a disproportionate or overly harsh way, I reminded myself that they might be having a completely unconscious response activated by past trauma, and that I should be able to have grace for that. In other words: it was easier for me to see that people were doing the best they could with what they had.

And along the way, I started to issue a little bit of grace to myself, recognizing that none of this is easy.

Chapter 8

WHAT GOES IN MUST COME OUT

Above all else, guard your heart, for everything you do flows from it.

—Proverbs 4:23

I used to mainline the news.

I was a straight-up junkie. It didn't matter how terrible it made me feel or how amped up I got, I just needed more. Yes, being informed about what is happening in the world is key to my job, but the minute-by-minute consumption of political news—much of it on Twitter and other social media platforms—was never necessary for my work.

As I would learn, it was actually counterproductive.

Most of the news I consumed was through my phone, which provided a nonstop flurry of notifications about new emails, texts, news stories, and people messaging me on social media. Many people I know live this way. I was incessantly checking Twitter and Instagram and engaging in something I later learned is called "doom scrolling," where you can't stop following an unfolding controversy on social media, no matter how dirty you feel after you do it.

In a 2020 *New York Times* story, a Smith College student

lamented the insane amount of time she had spent watching two beauty bloggers call each other out. "It just fires something emotionally," she said. "There's like a dopamine trigger that makes me keep scrolling."[1] The weirdest part? She didn't even like makeup tutorials.

It's not "like" a dopamine trigger. It *is* a dopamine trigger. Social media is designed to hook us and keep us on the platform for as long as possible.

"It's as if [social media companies] are taking behavioral cocaine and just sprinkling it all over your interface and that's the thing that keeps you . . . coming back and back and back," former Mozilla employee Aza Raskin told the BBC in 2018.[2] "Behind every screen on your phone, there are . . . literally a thousand engineers that have worked on this thing to try to make it maximally addicting." Raskin is credited with helping design "infinite scroll," which loads content continuously so the user can—and often does—scroll or swipe endlessly without having to click on anything. "If you don't give your brain time to catch up with your impulses," Raskin said, "you just keep scrolling."

This turns popular social media apps like Facebook, Twitter, and Instagram into black holes where we log in to see a picture of our friend's baby and two hours later find ourselves disoriented and unable to account for how we spent that time. "Nothing holds our attention better than the unknown," wrote digital entrepreneur Yazin Akkawi in a *Medium* post about smartphone addiction.[3] "A bottomless stream of social media posts motivates you to continue the search for the element of surprise; seeking things that captivate, engross, and entertain."

As with any drug, the more social media you consume, the more you want—even if it leaves you tired, distressed, and on edge. If I wanted to have any hope of practicing grace, I needed to get a handle on my social media addiction.

Nowhere was my condemning, self-righteous evil twin more

likely to show up than on Twitter. For journalists, Twitter is a constant lure in the way I suppose Facebook is for many other people. Like most social media, Twitter was once a fairly benign place where people would share articles and connect with like-minded users. Over time, it's become, much like Facebook, a cesspool of misinformation, brutal takedowns, and harassment. If you aren't locked in to binary thinking already, you will be after ten minutes on Twitter. The people who get the most attention have a single-minded focus on prosecuting their cases and destroying those who believe the "wrong" things. The nastier you are, the better. On Twitter, I could be snarky, self-righteous, and insufferable—all while being completely unaware of the emotional pain rustling deep inside me that I had tried to medicate with distraction, drama, and aggression toward "bad" people.

Of course, nearly every Twitter junkie has a high-minded rationale for their addiction. Members of the media follow what's happening on Twitter to gauge how politicians, other journalists, and activists are reacting to the news. But only 22 percent of U.S. adults say they are on Twitter. An even smaller percentage are regularly churning out information and opinions about politics. "The Twitter conversation about national politics . . . is driven by a small number of prolific political tweeters," noted Pew Research Center in late 2019. "These users make up just 6 percent of all U.S. adults with public accounts on the site, but they account for 73 percent of tweets from American adults that mention national politics." Pew found that just 13 percent of overall tweets during a one-year period ending in 2019 were related specifically to politics.[4]

Deep down, I knew all this. I knew Twitter presented at best a distorted and narrow view of the greater American conversation and at worst a negation of good-faith dialogue. Since I was working to unlearn the binary way I experienced the world, I thought it might help if I dialed down my Twitter use—and on weekends I'd declared it off-limits. I was making some progress on following my new guidelines when one Saturday in January 2019, I made an exception and clicked on a link a friend had emailed me.

I was immediately transported into the maw of a raging online battle. It doesn't matter what the controversy was, because it could have been about anything. Losing hours of my day arguing with people who seemed committed to misunderstanding me was nothing new. This is the way of Twitter, and I doubt it's by accident. Serious issues are broached in 280-character tweets, whereupon people use the retweet button to alert everyone that someone has expressed an opinion that warrants a righteous pile-on.

I had gone down this road so many times, and it always ended the same way: with me feeling dirty and gross about my own behavior and also angry and exhausted by other people's. Inevitably, by the end I'd be receiving threatening tweets, Facebook messages, and emails. To paraphrase Neil Young, I'd seen the needle and the damage done.

So this time I walked away, right? Nope. I continued to engage in entirely fruitless exchanges with conservatives who merrily twisted my original argument beyond recognition. There I was, once again strung out on the drug that always left me feeling like garbage. It wasn't the first time I had felt this way, but it would be the last.

Finally, I made one good decision: I deleted the Twitter app from my phone. I did it in the way I imagine alcoholics empty bottles of vodka down the drain to avoid succumbing to their lure.

This one seemingly minor act paid larger dividends than I could ever have imagined.

The personal benefits were immediate. I started to feel calmer and less agitated in a matter of days. The hours I used to spend on Twitter I now devoted to integrating other health-

ier practices into my life like meditation, centering prayer, jour-
naling, and hiking to connect with nature. I felt more grounded
and present in my offline (real) life.

I decided to use the time for self-reflection and be more in-
tentional about what had been up to that point an unstructured
consideration of my nuance-lacking contributions to the public debate. I began to look back over my past work with fresh
eyes. I didn't like what I found.

My over-the-top rhetoric or blindingly black-and-white "hot
takes" made me cringe. I had spent too much time perched
upon a high horse, dispensing self-righteous proclamations.
Like Holly Hunter in the iconic 1980s movie *Broadcast News,* I
was bereft of self-awareness and lamenting how lonely it felt to
always know better than everyone else. Driving home the point
that a dose of humility was due, I realized that I now wholly
rejected some of these obnoxiously self-certain opinions of
the past. Unfortunately, there they were, on the Internet forever.

Initially it was hard to reconcile my more regrettable comments with the fact that most of the time I was seen as a level-
headed, logic-driven columnist and on-air analyst. I had so
often been called "the voice of reason" by colleagues, viewers,
readers, and friends that it could have been on my business
card. Weeks of self-recrimination followed this harsh new self-
assessment, until a friend interrupted my shame spiral by pointing out that I was still engaging in the same kind of dualism
that had caused me so many problems. I was reminded of the
"both/and": I could be *both* an insightful analyst *and* a person
who behaved less than admirably at times.

My lack of grace for myself as I pursued the project of trying to bring more of it into the world was not lost on those
around me. "*Where's the grace for Kirsten?*" became a common
refrain in my world. Still, I longed for a delete button with
which I could simply vaporize some of my past public pro-

nouncements and start over afresh. I saw a geyser of what Christian author Philip Yancey calls "ungrace," despite my professed beliefs in a faith tradition that practically treats the hymn "Amazing Grace" as its anthem.

Once I had broken my Twitter habit (after a month or so), I allowed myself to venture back on, but only on my computer. I don't know if the addictive spell had been broken, or if the lack of "infinite scroll" really was the difference—maybe it was both—but I noticed I had almost no interest in what was happening there.

I had gone back on to post a Twitter thread about what I had discovered during my brief hiatus. I shared that I was beginning to realize how out of control and toxic our political realm had become, even before Trump came on the scene. We were a culture in desperate need of grace.

"I work hard to see every side of an issue and also speak up when I see a wrong," I wrote. "But in doing that I am too often judgmental and condemning—both on and off social media—in a way that is contrary to my belief system and my faith. I want to stand on the side of justice and equality but also of grace and I have failed to do that. Part of grace is recognizing my own fallibilities and imperfect judgment and reminding myself that there but for the grace of God go I."[5] I ticked off some examples where I felt I had lacked grace toward both conservatives and liberals.

I'd love to say that I was swarmed only by well-wishers. But this was still Twitter, after all.

"Pure liberal bullshit!" tweeted one dissatisfied customer. "You can never do better as long as you are blinded by that flawed ideology." Another ostensibly Christian man wrote, "Spend more time pondering who your master really is. I heard you reflect on finding God many times. Seek him. The media is lost and you are on the wrong path. Ponder that."

My *USA Today* editor saw the Twitter thread and suggested I write a column, and so I did. I acknowledged my role in our toxic culture and pledged to do better. I was setting down a marker for myself that this would be a true turning point. Making a public apology served not only as an act of personal accountability for my past behavior, but also as a pledge about my future behavior. After years of dualistically "othering" and even demonizing, I was at long last turning to grace.

In seeking to achieve this goal, I was increasingly realizing that the dualistic nature of the media in general, and social media in particular, was a great impediment. So I maintained my ban on the Twitter app for the foreseeable future. I turned off all notifications on my phone except for texts, so I wouldn't be enticed to check my email routinely or tap on a news alert that would just lead me down a rabbit hole.

I stopped watching television news altogether. I curated my Instagram so that my feed only showed accounts of friends, inspiring quotes, cute puppy videos, and beautiful and stylish pictures of Jennifer Aniston (yes, I'm obsessed). It wasn't completely politics-free, because so many of my friends are politically aware or are activists, but at least I wasn't relying on accounts that pushed outrage to drive traffic. To stay informed, I read news stories but set a timer to keep my consumption to no more than an hour, unless I had to read more for work. I stayed away from all opinion writing.

My friends, however, did not stop talking to me about the latest outrages, often texting news stories or even screenshots of tweets. It had long been our practice to exchange articles and social media posts and bond over how much we hated the same people. Still, even a few sentences were enough to get me activated. I'd feel my heart start to race and disgust well up in me. So, I issued a ban on this practice as well, knowing that I could be informed without inviting misery.

It must seem strange to have someone who makes her living in the news business telling you to cut and curate your news consumption. But it's just common sense that if you spend an inordinate amount of your day hearing about what is wrong in the world, you are going to be agitated and fearful, at best. And it's hardly a secret that journalism is in many ways driven by conflict and the promotion of bad behavior. A little of this goes a long way. Too much of it, and offering grace to others, or even yourself, becomes much more difficult.

"It is possible that someone's nervous system can be over-whelmed by seeing all the bad news on TV and on the internet [and] that this person may develop trauma symptoms," On-site's Austin Houghtaling told me.[6] "Furthermore, if someone has previously untreated and unintegrated or unprocessed trauma from earlier in life, current events [might] re-traumatize or activate them. I think our nervous systems are under attack frequently. Hence, the need to develop appropriate self-care practices and healthy support."

This means that even if you don't have prior trauma, or you have integrated previous trauma, your body could experience nonstop blasts of conflict and bad news as trauma. At a mini-mum, it's chronic stress. It's hard to feel grounded and con-nected to yourself and others when your body is being constantly activated by the geyser of negative information aimed at it.

While you may be convinced you are merely being a solid citizen by obsessively staying on top of the political news, it isn't necessarily so. A voluminous, round-the-clock intake of political information doesn't guarantee that you'll be well in-formed; in fact, steady consumption of bias-confirming data points likely narrows your perspective. Social scientists warn about the "paradox of information access." As we gain access to more and more information, we are "exposed to increas-ingly narrower bands of the ideology spectrum. Societies get fragmented into increasingly ideologically isolated enclaves. These enclaves (or echo-chambers) then become vulnerable to misinformation spread, which in turn further magnifies polarization and bias."[7]

According to a study from the organization More in Common, compared to the national average, the people who post about politics on social media have a higher perception gap.[8] This means they have a particularly distorted understanding of those with opposing political persuasions—and it's true regardless of political or ideological orientation. People's perception gaps will draw them to post stories and information that buttress their beliefs about the other side and support the caricatures they hold. And because social media rewards incendiary "us against them" posts far more than those that are tame and nuanced, there is an incentive, conscious or not, to continue providing this kind of content to rack up "likes" and "shares."

It should also come as no surprise that the people who have the most distorted views about those in opposing camps constitute the most ideologically fervent wings—what the More in Common survey labeled "progressive activists" and "devoted conservatives." They can inadvertently attract people who are unconsciously drawn to what Brené Brown calls "common enemy intimacy," in which we bond to each other over our shared hatred of the same people. When we are high on this kind of bonding, the ideas of compassion, empathy, mercy—and, yes, grace—are often dismissed as weak-kneed accommodation of the enemy and a betrayal of the community.

None of this is to say that you should disbelieve everything you see on social media or that every person who posts about politics is perpetrating stereotypes and "othering" those with whom they disagree. Some who post may possess authoritative insight into opposing political or ideological groups because they have done the research or may even have formerly belonged to the opposing group and have firsthand knowledge. Those who lack such expertise or have failed to dig deep into the information they are sharing aren't necessarily setting out to deceive. In all likelihood, they sincerely believe the faulty information they're spreading.

I want to make clear that social media is not all bad. It can be *both* a source of misery *and* a tool for justice. Twitter was the rocket fuel that propelled *both* Donald Trump and the white supremacist alt-right *and* the social movements Black Lives Matter and Me Too. Without social media, it's hard to imagine we would have had increased accountability for police brutality and sexual assault and harassment.

We just have to be realistic about the ways an overdependence on social media for political information can misshape our views. As I discussed in Chapter 4, our recent tendency to sort ourselves into like-minded communities has meant that fewer and fewer of us have actual relationships with people who think differently than we do. Where, then, does a Democrat learn what a Republican believes, and vice versa? Increasingly, it's from our chosen politician, pundit, and social media influencer—who, it turns out, often provides the *least* accurate assessment of what actual members of the opposing group are thinking. As the Northwestern University political scientist James N. Druckman told me, "The emergence of social media and emphasis on the extremes in the mainstream media leaves people with vast misperceptions of the other side. So, we think of the other side in the abstract and we characterize them as remarkably different: extreme, demographically distant, hostile, and antidemocratic."[9]

Again, some of these high-octane binary thinkers earnestly believe what they're spouting. Others, however, are what Harvard social scientist Arthur Brooks calls "rhetorical dope peddlers"[10] and the journalist Amanda Ripley has dubbed "conflict entrepreneurs."[11] These individuals thrive on partisan news outlets and social media, throwing red meat to people who are already revved up and ready to go on the attack about the next outrage. Their goal is not to inform; it is to rile people up to drive clicks, ratings, or get attention for themselves or their political cause. *Caveat emptor!*

Not without reason, the public is quick to find fault with the media. In August 2020, Gallup and the Knight Foundation released a survey that showed 83 percent of Americans blame the media for political division in this country. Forty-seven percent said the media bear "a great deal" of the blame, and another 36 percent pinned "a moderate amount" of the blame on the media. A majority of Americans believe that there is political bias in news coverage. Fifty-seven percent "see at least a fair amount of bias in their go-to news source." But what caused the overwhelming majority of them the greatest concern? The media diet of *other people*. Sixty-four percent of the respondents were more concerned about other people consuming biased news media than they were about their own news being biased.[12]

As much as we like to point to those who are feeding the other side lies about us and the world, the rhetorical dope peddlers we need to be most on the lookout for are the ones who share our own worldview and stand to benefit from making us despise other people. But like a fish that doesn't know it's wet, if you are flooding your system with biased media daily, you probably aren't aware of it. In my experience, the people who consume vast amounts of partisan news often believe they have found the only people who actually tell the truth. They're trapped in what conservative author Jonah Goldberg calls "bubble fortification," a mentality in which people have seized upon their preferred narrative, decided they've made up their minds and "don't care about the evidence, or facts, or consequences anymore."[13]

Meanwhile, there's overwhelming evidence that tuning out the news and logging off your favorite social media app might actually help you see your ideological foes more clearly. The More in Common survey found that the people with the most accurate understanding of what political opponents actually believe are the politically disengaged.[14] Perhaps that's because they aren't consuming the daily diet of demonization that nourishes so many people in the ideological wings of each party.

So, I'll offer a test for you to discern whether you have fallen under the sway of a rhetorical dope peddler. After you consume news, you should feel more informed, not more activated to demonize other people. If your regular reaction after you check your favorite news source or social media platform is to feel contempt or hatred for people on the "other side," then you need to find a new way to stay informed. It's one thing to be upset or angry about the actions of other people; it's another thing to see a person or group of people as beneath consideration or worthless. Even being angry on a daily basis, however justified, means that your system is being constantly stressed. Consider dialing down your consumption or try different outlets or mediums through which to consume news.

Learn to recognize healthy concern and engagement versus unhealthy "othering." We should never lose our capacity to be outraged about injustice or stop being concerned about what's happening in the world. But be sure to take note of the flavor of your outrage. Is it the kind that inspires you to take a concrete action to address an injustice or wrong? Or is your outrage just another opportunity to prove you are better than other people? It's easy to mistake posting nasty comments on social media for activism.

Therapist Courtney Leak says that whenever she sees someone on social media tearing another person down, she wants to tell them, "How you show your outrage is proportionate to your wellness. Until you have done some work, be quiet on a public forum."[15]

She isn't talking about people who use social media constructively to draw attention to important issues, or even to call out a person or organization that is causing harm. She's referring to people who are ripping others to shreds, speaking to and about people with contempt, or riling up their followers to pile on another person for saying something offensive. She contrasts this kind of behavior with a call to action with constructive solutions, such as using the hashtag "MuteRKelly" to hold the R&B singer accountable for his sexual abuse of young Black women.

You should also examine whether you feel you "need" to check your favored news outlet or social media every hour or few hours. That's a "tell," as they say in poker, that you are addicted to the dopamine hit. If we're being honest, many of us turn to social media or the news to be entertained, distracted, or numbed, not to become better citizens. We've become a reality TV–obsessed nation that often rewards people for the most toxic and immature behavior, even when discussing important issues.

Notice that I am not saying you should stop following the daily news cycle. I'm saying you should not overindulge. Each person should conduct their own experiment and notice at what point news consumption begins to affect their mental health and view of the world and other people. Always keep in mind that whatever you take in is going to have to go out. If you keep yourself in a constant state of agitation, you will take it out on either yourself or someone else. You can only imbibe so much information that upsets you before it manifests itself emotionally or physically.

We simply are not designed to bear the burdens of the entire world minute by minute or hour by hour. Our biologically built-in negativity bias—a function that gave our ancestors a heightened sense of awareness of predatory threats and natural dangers—has now hit its evolutionary wall. And even as our fatigued brains continue to seek out negativity, the "if it bleeds, it leads" media increasingly and deliberately supply it.

A seventeen-country study published in the official journal

of the National Academy of Sciences in late 2019 found that "all around the world, the average human is more physiologically activated by negative than by positive news stories." This is why you can't say no to that link promising to show you a smackdown of someone you don't like. The study also noted that "concerns about media coverage typically focus on the supply side of the media—i.e., choices of journalists and editors—but the demand side may be equally important. Even as people say they want more positive news, they systematically select more negative news."[16]

The good news is that you have significant control over the demand side. You can make a decision to change what you let into your head. Turn off your notifications, limit your news and social media consumption, and stay away from the rhetorical dope peddlers. You can trade in the sugar high of feeding your negativity bias and create space for more grace in your life right now.

Chapter 9

JUST SAY NO

Boundaries define . . . what is me and what is not me.
A boundary shows me where I end and someone else begins.

—Henry Cloud[1]

Seared into my memory is a day when my mother arrived home from work, worn out as usual. I ran to her, desperate to tell her about something that had upset me at school so she could offer me comfort.

Her reply left eight-year-old me in tears. "I just can't deal with this when I get home!" she snapped. With my younger brother looking on, she explained that she had to put up "boundaries" with us. One of these would be, she said, that when she arrived home at the end of the day, we each had five minutes to tell her anything that was wrong. After that, she didn't want to hear any more. Already I'd felt she had a wall around her that was impossible to penetrate. Now she was putting a name on the thing I hated the most: her emotional unavailability.

Anxiety and terror surged through my little body, and a lifelong hatred of boundaries was born.

In hindsight, I can see that this led to all sorts of dysfunctional relationships in every realm of my life. Throughout adulthood I managed to make some critical friendships with healthy people, but I was also constantly orbited by a succession of misfit toys who would behave in outrageous and unhealthy ways while I looked the other way. I never confronted the behavior—I was a misfit toy, too, so who was I to judge? Instead, I would seethe with resentment until some minor incident would start World War III, and the friendship would end. Before long, another problematic person would take their spot.

One day, a decade and a half ago, my friend Jamal tried to help me understand what I was doing. Speaking of one charismatic but emotionally unpredictable friend who had acted out the night before, he said, "You know how on sitcoms sometimes there is a recurring guest, sometimes from another sitcom?"

"Yeah," I said, not sure where this was going.

"Well, Nancy's supposed to be a guest star, not part of the regular cast," he explained. "She's someone you invite to your Christmas party, not talk to every day."

I thought I was just giving people grace. But really, I had no boundaries. Nor did I want them.

What a disappointment it was, then, to learn a few years ago that boundaries were so integral to practicing grace. Moreover, it became clear that I had internalized a flawed interpretation of boundaries from my frazzled young mother, who was just trying to survive managing a career and raising two young children with little money and no margins for error as a woman forging a career in the 1970s.

After explaining to me how boundaries are actually meant to be practiced, my therapist suggested that rather than demonizing and judging all the people who were making me so angry in this era of "alternative facts," I could use boundaries. If I did this, she explained, I would feel less activated by their behavior, which was sapping me of my energy and making me miserable.

She also informed me it was possible to be empathetic without carrying the world's problems on my shoulders.

I was skeptical, to say the least.

Many people who live in near-constant states of agitation and agony about what is going on in the world, or the problematic views or behavior of other people, believe their upset is proof of how much they care. I certainly did. I thought my sadness and anxiety were the price I had to pay for being empathetic. But the truth is, we don't have to suffer to prove we care about other people. We don't have to be perpetually angry and spun up about others' behavior to be engaged.

It's wonderful to be empathetic, and we need more empathy in the world. But what many of us call empathy is actually just an open door policy to toxic behavior that leaves us burned out.

I belatedly learned that boundaries create a buffer between us and the behavior and beliefs of other people. They help us navigate the world in an emotionally grounded and productive manner. They protect our energy, emotional health, and even physical well-being. When we use boundaries, we do not give away our power to other people to hijack our day, week, or month with their behavior.

In addition to helping us see other people through a lens of grace, boundaries help us have grace for *ourselves*.

"There is a 'me' in every situation that needs to be seen and respected, and you need to remember that *you* are doing the best you can with what you have," notes Dr. John Draper, a psychologist and one of the country's leading suicide-prevention experts (and my fiancé's brother).[2] The moment you decide to use boundaries is the moment you cut yourself some slack and start saying no to things that drain or agitate or scare you. You no longer become entangled in other people's dramas. You know that you matter and deserve to be treated well, and that the people who are driving you nuts don't have a right to unrestrained access to you.

Once I understood just how transformative boundaries were, I was immediately converted.

My therapist explained boundaries in very simple terms: decide what you are a "no" to, and whenever anyone engages in that kind of behavior, let them know it's not okay, or if you prefer you can just change the subject or end the conversation. You don't need to demonize or get in an argument or seethe with resentment because someone keeps doing the same thing you are a "no" to over and over.

I am a "no" to contempt, cruelty, disrespect, shaming, judging, bad-faith accusations, bullying, gaslighting, demonizing, dehumanizing, lying, both-sides-ism (creating false equivalency between the behavior of different people or groups), and any and all forms of bigotry. I am a "no" to having conversations with people who are committed to misunderstanding me.

Being clear about my boundaries meant I stopped wasting precious energy on the people who crossed them. The first boundaries I set were around the kind of information and how much of it I would allow into my life via social media and the news media. Later on, I learned how to institute boundaries at work and in my personal life.

Using boundaries doesn't mean that you don't confront people when they have caused harm. It doesn't mean you don't argue against bad ideas. By all means, speak your truth! It means that you resist the pull of hatred—since the moment we go that route, we have allowed what we oppose "to invade our inner light," as the civil rights legend Ruby Sales told me.[3] "Once you hate, you are no longer in control of your destiny," she said. Boundaries put emotional and psychological space between ourselves and the behavior and beliefs of other people.

Every person has a different capacity for (or interest in) conflict. Some people really love to get into vigorous debates. They aren't bothered when a debate or argument turns combative, and even nasty. Others need disagreement to stay calm and measured. You have to decide what works for you and develop your boundaries based on that.

One word of warning for people who have not used boundaries in the past, and especially those who have not processed their trauma: the inclination can be to swing to the opposite extreme and create overly rigid boundaries where there once were none. This can look like demonizing and cutting out any person who expresses an opinion you don't like or defining anyone who does something upsetting to you as "unsafe." People with overly rigid boundaries might start labeling family members and friends "toxic" and reflexively discarding them when approaching the relationships with more finely calibrated boundaries might be the solution.

Boundaries aren't meant to turn you into an impenetrable fortress. Ideally, they should show people how to interact or be in relationship with you. In my experience, most people are happy to have this information. The only people who were resistant to me instituting boundaries were those who were benefitting from me not having them in the first place. In those cases, I did have to step away from the relationship.

When I say I'm a "no" to certain behaviors, that doesn't mean I'm a "no" to any person who exhibits them. If someone tries to engage in a conversation with me using a "both sides" argument to shift focus from the responsible party, I just change the topic. I don't deem that person toxic or bad. In my experience, it's when you don't use boundaries that your resentment grows so much that you begin to view people who are merely annoying or unpleasant as dangerous or unsafe.

If we want to practice grace with challenging people, we need to be focused on creating internal emotional safety, because external emotional safety is simply unachievable. We can't control how other people behave. The more integrated we become, the more our capacity grows to engage with people who in the past activated us. That said, the fact that you have the capacity to deal with someone doesn't mean you are obligated to do so. Life is short. You have a right to spend your energy the way you want. And lest there be any confusion: there *are* people who are unsafe and psychologically dangerous, and you should be wary of being in relationship with them and use strong boundaries if you must interact with them.

I'll give you an example of how using boundaries has worked in my life. At Robert's father's funeral in late 2019, his Trump-supporting aunt informed me accusingly that I worked for "fake news." I just stared at her. Does something like that require a response, at a funeral or elsewhere? I won't spend my energy on things like this. At this point, I actually had the emotional capacity to engage her without it affecting me, but I had no interest in doing so. I said nothing, and she was left with an awkward silence to fill. In another instance, I have a family member who likes to gossip about other family members and won't stop despite being asked to repeatedly. So now when it happens, I just say, "You need to discuss that with them. I can't help." Then I change the subject. I no longer seethe over having to listen to things I didn't want to hear, which would cause me to resent this family member. I've found also that using boundaries helps me stay grounded. When I'm clear about where I stand, I don't feel like I'm at the mercy of other people's behavior.

In both cases, I am showing grace to myself by taking care of my emotional needs and not pushing myself to engage in situations that will sap my energy. I am also showing grace to the other person rather than snapping at or demonizing them, which is both kind and keeps me from becoming entangled in their stories. They are going to say what they want to, but I don't have to participate.

So, sometimes your boundary is that you won't even entertain a conversation. Other times, you will have the conversation but with certain guardrails in place about what type of conversation you will have. When someone violates a boundary you have set, you let them know. If they won't respect your boundary, then you can end the conversation. If a person repeatedly ignores your boundaries, you might want to reassess the relationship and possibly redefine it. In some cases, such as a person who repeatedly violates your boundary that you won't be yelled at, you might need to end the relationship.

In addition to knowing what we are a "no" to, we should be clear about what we are a "yes" to. I'm a "yes" to respectful dialogue and debate, constructive criticism, honesty, good-faith debates, humility, kindness, and support for justice and equality. This is not an all-encompassing list but is just meant to give you a sense of the kinds of things to consider when determining what you want to allow in your life.

Many of us end up being activated and upset by people we don't even know personally. We can't call the senator who is lying and tell him that he's violating our boundaries and needs to stop lying. But we *can* say "no" when that politician comes on television. We can say "no" to allowing this person to invade our inner light. Just press mute, change the channel, or turn off the TV. Don't give prime real estate in your brain to someone who doesn't deserve it.

What might your "yes" look like? In this case, it might mean volunteering or donating to a campaign to defeat the lying senator. In another scenario, it might mean donating money to an organization that works to end the harm that has been brought to your attention. It could be working to raise awareness about the issue by posting information on social media and sharing it widely with people you know who are aligned with your values. For me, it might be screaming into a pillow and then writing a column. (No, I'm not joking.)

When it comes to being activated by something you see in the news or on social media, use boundaries instead of melting down. This doesn't mean you don't have feelings or don't get angry. Anger can be a good thing. It lets you know something is wrong. We should never lose our capacity to be outraged. We just want it to propel us toward embracing our "yes" instead of being dragged low by our "no."

"Even the most egregious thing said by another person you don't know shouldn't have the power to unhinge you, unless it's attached to previous wounding," Courtney Leak explained to me. "If we can heal those woundings, these incidents don't harm us as much. Even when they involve very triggering issues such as racism and other bigotry, we can express how we feel about it while staying within ourselves because it's not tethered to our wounding."[4]

Leak says the way she feels as a Black woman is "The racists don't deserve my energy. I've been harmed enough. Doing my work and being well is an act of resistance against people who would dehumanize me. Racists don't want me to feel safe, valued, and feel joy. Having love and connection and creating safety for myself are acts of resistance."

This is what it looks like to use boundaries as an act of grace for yourself.

How might boundaries work in a situation where you have to confront differing political views or values? Here's an example: Susan is on her second date with Jim when he mentions he voted for and supports Donald Trump. Susan is a Republican, but she believes Trump is a demagogue and is still seething over the fact that he never conceded the election. Dating a Trump supporter is a "no" for her. (It might not be for someone else, but it is for her.)

Susan (option one): You did *what*? What kind of person would do such a thing? I can't date someone with such bad character. I don't ever want to see you again.

Susan (option two): Wow, that's a surprise. I enjoyed our last date, but I'm a definite "no" to Donald Trump and can't date someone who supports him. We're just not a good fit.

The first option is full of judgment and by using it Susan

immediately gets emotionally entangled with Jim's views and beliefs, which is a waste of her energy, especially since she has no plans to see him again. She judges him by attacking his character. Whether she is right or wrong in her assessment is not the point. What matters is that Susan has let Jim hijack her emotions, even if that probably wasn't his intention.

The second reaction uses boundaries, and it is a more graceful response. Jim may not like the fact that Susan is not going to see him again, or that she disapproves of voting for Trump, but she spoke up about what's important to her without attacking his character or judging him. For Susan's sake, she can walk away from this situation and move toward her "yes," which is finding a person to date who is more aligned with her worldview. Susan has been clear about the fact that Jim's views belong to him, not her, all while treating him respectfully.

By the way, all of this advice could just as easily be applied by a strong Trump supporter who discovers their date despises their hero. It's probably needed advice: a 2020 survey showed that 63 percent of respondents, regardless of political party, had no interest in dating a person with differing views about Donald Trump.[5]

When we don't let people know what our boundaries are, or when we fail to enforce them, we end up becoming resentful. The more our resentment builds, the more likely we will begin to see others as inherently bad, rather than as people with bad beliefs or bad behavior. Before I learned how to use boundaries, my body was a cauldron of resentment, always ready to boil over. I was much more likely to snap at someone or become visibly agitated when discussing contentious issues. This was unpleasant for me, and it also undermined whatever point I was trying to make.

For years, I seethed about men constantly interrupting me on TV. More often than not, I'd be the only woman on what I came to refer to as "manels." When one of the men would inevitably interrupt me after I had barely gotten out a full sentence, I would say things like "Let me finish," which occasionally would stop them. But since I never held anyone accountable for crossing that boundary, they naturally kept interrupting me. Meanwhile, people on social media would complain about the interruptions, and my fiancé, Robert, would be enraged on my behalf.

One evening following a CNN appearance, a woman on Twitter gave me a tip: "Don't say 'let me finish' because you are asking for permission to finish your sentence. Tell them to stop interrupting you." From then on, that's what I did. Sometimes I would stop completely, stare at the person, and say, "I'm talking. Why did you start talking in the middle of my sentence?" Other times I would say firmly, "Don't interrupt me" or "Stop interrupting me." The problem never went completely away, but when I started making clear that I wouldn't tolerate this manel energy, the interruptions reduced significantly, and so did my seething. Later, I noticed my CNN colleague Laura Coates coolly informing a manterrupter, "I *will* finish my sentence," and I filed this quip away for future use.

Another boundary I instituted was that I would not discuss politics with Trump surrogates unless we were on air and I was doing it as part of my job. When we were off set, politics was a no-go zone. When they'd try to engage me in a political conversation in the greenroom or while we were getting our makeup done, I'd change the subject. If they persisted, I'd say, "I only talk about this when I'm on the clock." Only one of them ignored these boundaries, and if you are a CNN watcher, you probably know who it is. He would continue the on-air disagreement all the way out of the studio, into the elevator, and out of the doors of the building. No amount of silent treatment or telling him I didn't want to talk about politics with him when we were off air would make a difference. So, I instituted a new approach. When we finished our segment, I would remain in my chair long enough to know that by the time I came out, he'd already be in the elevator.

The more I embraced boundaries, the less I was jammed up with contempt. I began to feel a growing capacity for grace. I no longer left the studio feeling enraged by what I had to listen to. I heard what people said, I disagreed, and then I left. By recognizing where I ended and other people began, I learned to stop at "no" and not go down the road of labeling their behavior, judging them, or hating them. When people brought up Donald Trump outside of work, I would raise my hand to stop them and explain that I didn't talk about him unless it was for my job.

You'll recall from Chapter 2 how that edict was first put to the test when I ordered my handyman friend Mark out of my house after he acknowledged being a Trump supporter. At that moment, I was constructing my personal boundaries on the fly. After apologizing for my insistence that Mark leave, I rebuffed his attempts to explain why he backed Trump because there was nothing he could say that would make me feel different, and based on the little conversation we had already had, it was pretty clear I wouldn't be able to move him. I had said what I had to say. Henceforth, we wouldn't discuss politics. That was my line in the sand, drawn for the sake of my own emotional well-being at that point in time. Today, I'd have capacity for this conversation, but back then I was hanging on by a thread and had zero energy to argue with another person about Trump.

Instituting boundaries meant I also stopped marinating in my grievances against other people. Doing that just compounds the problem. Not only have you experienced the unacceptable behavior, but you then find yourself thrashing through it with your friends and your partner—dissecting it, raging about it. You wake up at 3:00 A.M. replaying the scene, inserting all the zingers you wish you'd thought of at the time. Your anger and resentment take up residence in your body and manifest as chronic migraines or back pain. It doesn't have to be this way.

Just say no.

I'm not arguing against a healthy deconstruction of upsetting situations. But the reality is, once I started setting boundaries and dealt with much of my core trauma, I stopped needing to process so much with other people because I was so clear about what I was a "no" to. I wasn't interested in bringing that energy into my life.

Still, work colleagues or noxious politicians are one thing; family members are quite another. The latter can often be our most challenging relationships, replete as they are with lifelong grievances. Though family can be a person's ultimate refuge, it can also be a tinderbox ready to burst into an inferno from a single ill-fated comment.

If you want to remain in a relationship with family members—and most people do—you can't wait them out until they've headed to the elevator, as I did with my work colleague. They're a constant part of your life. Even so, you can draw boundaries around the kinds of conversations you are willing to have with them. You can recognize their behavior while not taking it on as your problem to fix or as a continuing object of offense that leaves you stewing for days.

Try establishing boundaries the next time your dad attempts to browbeat you into believing whatever he does about politics or religion. Even if what he's saying strikes you as dangerously misinformed, you don't need to take that on emotionally. If he's accusing "your side" of being immoral or intolerant or otherwise guilty of the grievance du jour, you don't need to defend yourself. Those are his issues, not yours.

Because the stakes are high when people hold beliefs that can cause harm to other people, there will be times where you feel duty-bound to engage. You should just be sure to use strong boundaries. Here are some examples of boundaries you could set:

"I'm willing to have this conversation, but it's not okay for you to use sarcasm or speak to me with contempt."

"It's okay for us to have different views about this. But unless you stop interrupting me, we can't continue this discussion."

"Rather than telling me what I, or other members of my political party, believe about immigration, why don't you ask me what I believe?"

"You can tell me how you feel right now, but it's not okay for you to yell or engage in name-calling."

"Please do not tell me what other members of the family are saying about my political or religious beliefs or share details about our disagreements with them."

Sometimes you can set the firmest boundaries imaginable and people like my CNN colleague will bust right through them anyway. These are emotionally unsafe people. Nothing you say is going to get them to engage with you in a healthy way.

When boundaries around behavior are repeatedly ignored, then it's time to say: "I don't want to discuss [insert issue] with you ever again." The issue could be anything: politics, religion, other family members, your romantic life, or viewpoints that cause division in your relationship or that you find offensive.

Sometimes people just aren't capable of mature disagreement, in which case it's best to avoid difficult conversations with them altogether. "Don't go to the hardware store to buy bagels," as the saying goes. A person can't give you something they don't have. If they persist in trying to pull you into a conversation you don't want to have, leave the room or hang up the phone. You are not obligated to have crazy-making conversations with anyone, including family.

Sometimes, people just want to argue. They aren't actually trying to understand you. We've all been there—in fact, it feels like some people are completely committed to misunderstanding you.

In the Sermon on the Mount, Jesus said, "Do not throw your pearls [before swine]. If you do, they may trample them under their feet, and turn and tear you to pieces."[6] No, this does not mean that anyone who criticizes you or picks a fight with you is swine. But pigs do not know that a string of pearls has any more value than a pile of dirt. Pigs will trample over both with the same disregard.

So it is with a person who just can't appreciate you or what you are saying. There is no point in expending your energy on such an individual. They may lack the curiosity, emotional maturity, or empathy to understand what you are saying. Not only is engaging with such a person a waste of your time, but it can be emotionally harmful for you, and can cause you to become increasingly agitated, angry, and resentful.

Grace becomes impossible in this state.

Underlying the idea of boundaries is something we all eventually learn: other people's behavior is not about you; it's about them. People accuse you of doing things that they do; they lash out and mistreat you because they are in pain, and so on. Which is why you should not get yourself pulled into other people's stories when they try to project them onto you.

Boundaries can be extra hard to maintain during family disputes because so many families are enmeshed, considering a sense of individuality separate from the family a betrayal. The family member who disrupts the enmeshment is not likely to have an easy go of it. Even a dysfunctional family resists changing its messed-up system. To challenge its structure is to threaten the family's very existence.

Which means, when you move away and become more liberal than your family and start talking to them about racial justice or feminism or less conservative interpretations of the Bible, you aren't just bringing up topics for discussion and debate. In their minds, it's an existential attack. The same thing happens if you come from a liberal atheist family and begin attending an evangelical church and talking about your Bible studies. (Trust me, I know.) If the family is healthy, they will find a way to navigate this new difference, even if it's difficult. But if the family is en-

meshed or dealing with other dysfunctions, the feelings of betrayal and confusion can be overwhelming.

Having empathy for your family's perspective will put you in
a better position to be graceful when disagreements erupt. But
the fact that you understand why your family is so upset doesn't
mean you have to participate in conversations that turn toxic,
or that you have to change or hide your beliefs to mollify them.
If their views harm you—like if you are an LGBTQIA person
and they believe homosexuality is a sin—you are not required
to listen to those views or even stay in a relationship with them.

I've watched how various gay friends who grew up in evangelical families have navigated this issue. When their families
say they won't allow them to bring their partners home for
Christmas, they choose not to go home. That's their boundary.
If the families relent and agree they can bring their partners
home for a holiday, it's usually with the caveat that the two can't
sleep in the same bedroom. So the couple either continues to
not go, or if they do, they stay in a hotel.

When their parents try to talk about how they are worried
my friends will go to Hell for their relationships, my friends all
have different responses. Some still engage and explain to their
parents why their religious beliefs are misinformed and harmful. Others refuse to have the conversation. One friend told his
father, "You are going to have to process your fear with someone else." Another friend, after endless heartbreak caused by
her family's rejection, has all but broken off contact with them
and instead relies on her chosen family of friends, who love
and accept her completely. These are all different versions of
boundaries.

Remember that setting expectations and limits about what
you will tolerate is meaningless without accountability. If you
tell your family—or anyone—that you have a boundary but
you let them cross it constantly, then it's not going to be effective. If you inform your mother you won't discuss politics with
her anymore but then indulge her the next time she brings the

subject up, you have only yourself to blame for the frustration you feel when you hang up the phone.

It's also important not to allow yourself to be guilt-tripped. You are doing nothing wrong when you refuse to have a conversation that feels toxic to you. Remind your family member that setting boundaries is an act of grace and love. When you use boundaries, you are leaning into a relationship instead of giving up on it. You are saying, "This relationship matters to me and I love you, but I can't have these kinds of conversations with you unless you adhere to some basic rules of engagement." You are also having grace for yourself, by recognizing that you don't have to consign yourself to misery if you and your family have deep disagreements. You deserve to have your needs or expectations honored. You are not required to have your peace disturbed—or in some cases, your humanity attacked—just because someone else wants to have an argument or express views you find problematic, offensive, or harmful.

These days, when I begin to feel that familiar panic or fury rising in my chest over what someone else has done, I remind myself that their behavior or views are not mine. I remind my self that I help nobody by melting down or becoming incapacitated by anxiety or worry. Overreacting, or even just reacting, doesn't prove I care. Likewise, when someone directs rage, judgment, or contempt at me, I tell myself, *That's theirs, not mine. Not my problem.*

Granted, these responses are not always immediate. Sometimes I still take the bait and begin to go down a path I regret. But more often than not these days, I can catch myself before I've taken on someone else's contempt, gaslighting, or anger.

The next time you see a pundit or politician expressing a view that makes you angry, frustrated, or anxious, try setting boundaries. Try it when dealing with a co-worker or neighbor who repeatedly shares ideological views with you that make your blood boil.

Just say no, then get to work on your "yes."

Chapter 10

CLOTHE YOURSELVES WITH HUMILITY

Pride makes us artificial and humility makes us real.
—THOMAS MERTON[1]

I saw a cartoon recently that summed up the way our brains work against us when it comes to fostering humility.

A man sitting at his computer says to himself, "I've heard the rhetoric from both sides. Time to do my *own* research on the real truth." His search brings up a result that says: "Literally the first link that agrees with what you already believe [and] supports your viewpoint without challenging it in any way" and a second option with the headline "Don't worry about this one." His mouse hovers over the first link as he says to himself, "Jackpot."[2]

Our brains are instinctually drawn to arguments that buttress our beliefs. This is known as "confirmation bias." I'm often accused of this bias when people are upset with my take on certain issues. The people making this criticism seem to believe that only those with whom they disagree engage in this behavior, and they are somehow above it.

Let me clear this up: we all do it. It's how we are wired. While it's *possible* you are right about everything, it's not very probable.

"The stories that we gravitate to are the ones that make sense to us, stories that fit, stories that feel like they have continuity, connection to the past, where we've been," Rev. Dr. Jacqui Lewis explains. "Those stories that we will follow are the ones that feel true . . . and that resonate with the trajectory of our lives. So, we're looking for the story that doesn't necessarily change our minds. We're actually looking for the story that confirms what's in our minds."[3]

In his 2021 book, *Think Again: The Power of Knowing What You Don't Know,* organizational psychologist Adam Grant included a pie chart showing the cognitive tools to which we mentally cling.[4] He lists assumptions, instincts, habits, and having an open mind. The chart is evenly divided among the first three—which is pretty concerning—but "having an open mind" didn't even merit the tiniest sliver of the pie. Most people believe they have adopted their views based on reasoned inquiry, research, and their own unique discernment. But social psychologist Jonathan Haidt warns, "We make our first judgments rapidly, and we are dreadful at seeking out evidence that might disconfirm those initial judgments."[5]

"Psychologists point out we are mental misers: we often prefer the ease of hanging on to old views over the difficulty of grappling with new ones," writes Grant. "Yet there are also deeper forces behind our resistance to rethinking. Questioning ourselves makes the world more unpredictable. It requires us to admit that the facts may have changed, that what was once right may now be wrong. Reconsidering something we believe deeply can threaten our identities, making it feel as if we're losing a part of ourselves."[6]

This probably explains why, when I reconsidered issues on which I had taken strong positions in the past, I felt so confused about my not having been aware of information that undermined my position. I had always done so much research, but I wasn't working to overcome my confirmation bias because back then I didn't even know such a thing existed.

If I'm being honest, for most of my life I looked at people who didn't share my worldview and wondered, *What is wrong with them? I've got all the facts right here. Why can't they see they are wrong and I'm right?*

This didn't leave a lot of room for grace.

It's really hard to override our bias that we are always right, but before we can have any hope of doing so, we have to develop intellectual humility—which Mark Leary, a social and personality psychologist at Duke University, defines as "the recognition that the things you believe in might in fact be wrong." This is a hard one for many people. I know it was for me. Leary says this kind of humility requires a "process of monitoring your own confidence."[7]

This means we need to actively pause at times and ask ourselves, "Am I missing something here?" or "Is it possible that my view is not the only way to see this situation?"

How often can you honestly say you do this?

I can tell you the amount of time I did this until fairly recently was close to zero. I was curious about others' views, but rarely did I integrate them into how I saw an issue or use that information to help me develop empathy for those who saw things differently. At the same time, I would have told you with 100 percent honesty that I was open to changing my mind about any issue if someone made a good argument. Of course, they somehow never did.

Intellectual humility is a radical notion in a society that views certainty as strength. As former president Bill Clinton has noted, "When people are feeling insecure, they'd rather have someone who is strong and wrong rather than somebody who is weak and right."[8] Donald Trump's propensity for bluster and exaggeration and his steadfast refusal to ever admit he's wrong further demonstrate how excessive pride is rewarded in our society.

Even if you have a developed sense of humility, it's difficult to express that humility in our punitive, "take no prisoners" culture. There's a reason politicians frequently refuse to apologize for past mistakes. They aren't *all* narcissists. They simply know that many Americans have been cajoled into viewing humility as proof of human weakness.

Never mind the frequent reminders that we are a country founded on Judeo-Christian values, invoking two religions that place a high premium on humility and repentance. "Pride goeth before destruction, and an haughty spirit before a fall," Proverbs warns.[9] Listening to many on the religious right, you would think Satan was kicked out of Heaven for being gay. But in the story from Genesis, it's the sin of pride that does him in. The New Testament is filled with warnings against pride and praise of humility, from Peter's declaration "God opposes the proud, but gives grace to the humble"[10] to Paul's instruction to clothe yourself with humility.[11]

Yet our public square is a desert of humility. This is where many Americans get their cues on how to handle disagreement, especially on contentious political issues, and suffice it to say the example being set isn't very inspiring. Certainty is rewarded, and nuance is discouraged.

My first newspaper column was for the *New York Post* covering the 2008 Democratic primary. After receiving a few drafts that offered "on the one hand, on the other hand" views, my editor shot me an email: "Pick a side. I don't care which side. Just pick it and make that argument." There just wasn't room in eight hundred words to weigh varying positions—and anyway, that wasn't what readers looked for when they opened the opinion section of the paper. Most editors I've worked with since have held the same view. Before you blame the media, understand that this mentality is driven by the consumer side of the ledger. It's often you, dear reader, who clicks on the link promising certainty and reinforcement of what you believe and blows by the more nuanced article that might challenge you.

We need to be aware of our psychological tendency to look at a situation and lock in on whatever supports our view while blinding us to any information that would challenge it. If we can do this, we might be able to change our media diets and seek out a broader range of views.

By all accounts, this behavior is unconscious—which is why it's usually a fool's errand to try to reason other people out of their beliefs. These efforts are pointless because the people didn't use reason to form their beliefs in the first place. Chances are, neither did we.[12]

People with strong partisan, religious, or ideological beliefs have to work extra hard at overcoming their unconscious bias. In a 2018 study, "The Partisan Brain," social scientists observed that "partisan identities alter information processing linked to reasoning, memory, implicit evaluation, and even perception." But people can apparently be shaken out of their trance if there is some accountability measure added in. The study noted that "paying [people] money for accurate responses can reduce partisan bias."[13]

It gives me some hope to know that we can overcome our biases and reflexive certainty if we are incentivized to do so. But no one is going to pay us to be accurate, so we will have to hold ourselves accountable. Understanding basic facts of brain science and psychology can help us monitor our own behavior and be less frustrated and judgmental when we see the same problematic behavior in other people.

In a May 2019 CNN segment, former U.S. senator Rick Santorum, a conservative Catholic, and I were discussing a controversial Alabama law that made abortion illegal at nearly any stage of pregnancy, would put doctors who performed abortions in prison, and offered no exception for rape or incest.[14] When host Anderson Cooper asked Santorum if it made sense that a doctor performing an abortion for a woman who had been raped might get more time in prison than the rapist, Santorum replied, "Well, yes, it does make sense, because we're ignoring the other person in the situation, and that's the child." He went on to defend this law, saying, Abortion "is wrong . . . Because you're killing a human being. And it's obvious to anybody because it's a fact."[15]

Of course, it's not obvious to everyone and it's not a fact. It's obvious to some people (usually those who hold it as a tenet of their Christian faith), but what Santorum described as obvious to "anybody" was in fact an opinion about a very complex topic.

Whether he intended to or not, his formulation—everyone can see that abortion is killing a person—implicitly cast anyone who supported abortion rights as a pretty bad person. I tried repeatedly to get him to acknowledge that there are people of good conscience who do not believe that an embryo is a person, including Jewish people who largely reject[16] conservative Christians' interpretation[17] of a verse in the Old Testament's Psalm 139 ("you created my inmost being; you knit me together in my mother's womb"[18]) as being about abortion. Santorum was unmoved and just kept reiterating his position.[19]

This exchange exemplifies the kind of intellectual and moral certainty too many of us possess about complicated issues. I certainly have been there. It's an instinct I've been trying to fight against for the past few years.

As with all problems, the first step is admitting that we *have* a problem. We need to get to a place where we can recognize that we may not fully understand every issue and that our brains are often working against us when we try to discern the truth of a situation or person. In addition to confirmation bias, our brains like to use shortcuts and engage in binary sorting, which leads to fast, but not necessarily accurate, conclusions.[20] Having such awareness should cause us to show humility when confronting issues or people. This is as true in politics as it is in our personal lives.

Grace creates space for us to do this kind of reflection. It helps us work to understand things from other people's perspectives, with empathy, and without compromising our own beliefs. Grace helps you accept the inherent tensions in life and recognize that as sure as you are that you have discerned the real truth about a situation or issue, you will never go wrong by allowing for the possibility that you don't know everything.

One barrier to empathy and understanding occurs when a person characterizes an ideological adversary's position in a way that is unrecognizable to the person who actually holds the view. David Blankenhorn, founder of Braver Angels—an organization that brings people from opposing sides of the political spectrum together in an effort to bridge the partisan divide—calls this "rhetorical framing," which is "describing your opponents' views with loaded words that your opponents themselves would never dream of using."[21]

In hindsight, I can see that myopic certainty and rhetorical framing were what led me down some very regrettable roads in my work. One area that I approached in an overly all or nothing way, devoid of all empathy and assumption of good faith, was my writing about free speech.

As I revisited my past work minus my binary blinders, I realized I had engaged in a sort of sacralizing of "free speech," treating it as the supreme value in society, which should have only the narrowest of limitations. Even when the speech was outrageously offensive and harmful, I saw this as the unfortunate price we had to pay to live in a society that protects speech. (When I use the term "free speech," I am not talking about government censorship; I am referring to societal pressure and punishment of people who express views deemed offensive or harmful.) I used to see free speech infringements behind every bush and was incapable of understanding the reasoning behind the desire to shut down certain speakers. I can see now that our ingrained propensity to seek out information that affirms our views, combined with my particular flavor of trauma, made having empathy or understanding regarding this issue a practical impossibility for me.

I wrote my first book, *The Silencing: How the Left Is Killing Free Speech* (how's that for a dualistic title?), in 2014, and it was published in mid-2015.[22] It was a critique of efforts to curb speech by people on the political left, making the case that doing so was against long-standing liberal values. For most of my life, the defenders of free speech had been lefty activists, whether on campus or at the ACLU. I took on the mantle of an old argument: that the only solution to bad speech is more speech.

With my growing understanding of my binary inclinations, I began to reconsider some of my core arguments about free speech and started rereading my book. I was taken aback at how dismissive and contemptuous I was toward those whom I believed were threatening other people's free speech. My arguments were completely lacking in empathy and, perhaps most importantly, humility. It simply did not occur to me that there was another way to see this issue, nor did I ever ask myself that critical question: "Am I missing something here?"

In one instance, where a white speaker had used the N-word at a 2012 Smith College alumni event in a discussion of whether *The Adventures of Huckleberry Finn* should be banned for its inclusion of the word, I criticized the ensuing controversy among students who said her behavior had been racist. While it's not something I ever would have said—indeed, it would have bothered me had I been present—I believed that because she didn't use the term in a derogatory manner and her intent was to make a point about the topic being discussed, the backlash against her was an attack on free speech.

Good Lord in Heaven. *I do not know who this person was who believed this.* I do not know this person who believed her opinion was equal to let alone superseded the opinions of the Black students complaining. It's true that back then there were plenty of white people who didn't consider what she did to be racist, and unfortunately some still hold this view, almost a decade after that event. But my lack of curiosity and humility was inexcusable. When I mentioned my horror about this to Robert, he said, "A debate between 2015 Kirsten and 2021 Kirsten would be one to watch." As the late British preacher Charles Spurgeon once noted, "If you are renewed by grace, and were to meet your old self, I am sure you would be very anxious to get out of [their] company."[23]

Indeed, in my book, I was utterly without grace. I sneered at trigger warnings and was dismissive of the idea that microaggressions are a phenomenon (they are). Because I usually shared the political and ideological values of the protesting students, I felt I had standing to weigh in on these topics. What I didn't consider is that I can be against homophobia all I want; what I can't do is know what it *feels* like when a homophobic speaker is invited to campus by fellow students. I also had no empathy for the students who had been sexually assaulted and felt activated when speakers came on campus to challenge sexual assault statistics. I had been sexually assaulted, after all, and I had no trouble listening to such arguments, whether I agreed with them or not.

Of course, I had zero realization at the time that part of the reason I didn't react to so many things was that I relied so heavily on the "flight" mechanism when trauma felt too overwhelming. That meant I would retreat into an emotionless, hyperanalytical approach and rely on "intellectualization," which is an emotional defense mechanism in which people use only reason and logic to understand a problem because they unconsciously want to avoid uncomfortable or distressing emotions, like remembering a sexual assault. I treated the topic of free speech like it was an algebra problem, not something that affects the basic dignity of human beings.

I also didn't understand at the time that many of these trau-

matized students might be having the "fight" response activated. This would make them desperately oppose a speaker
who they believed espoused harmful views from coming on
campus as a way to create a sense of psychological safety. This
doesn't mean the students are always right—sometimes they
are, and sometimes they aren't. It means they should be treated
with compassion, not contempt. When they show us they are
traumatized, they should be given access to support and healing, not treated to derision from their elders.

My lack of self-awareness concerning the issue of free
speech would be funny if it wasn't so tragic. Here I was essentially telling people to "calm down" and "stop being so emotional" and treating others with legitimate feelings, and
sometimes obvious unprocessed trauma, as though they were
completely irrational. It was ironically exactly how I had been
treated by my parents when I was a child. What many of these
students were doing was standing up for themselves, rather
than abandoning themselves, the way I had.

They are demonstrating what Rev. Dr. Martin Luther King
Jr. called "creative maladjustment." He explained in a 1967
speech, "There are some things concerning which we must always be maladjusted if we are to be people of good will."[24]
Some of these things, he said, were racial discrimination, religious bigotry, income inequality, militarism, and physical violence.

My generation ("X") was in some ways too adjusted to the
ways of the world. It's not that we didn't care—we just didn't
feel like we had much say in the matter. We complained about
sexism, racism, and every other "ism" in general terms, but most
of us knew that complaining specifically about our own treatment was a quick way to end up out of a job and difficult to
employ. There was no social media or Internet sites to post our
stories about sexual harassment, racism, and other discrimination or mistreatment. Something like #MeToo was completely

unimaginable. That powerful men would ever be held account-able for their abuse, let alone on such a large scale, was not a thought that could have been formed in my head. We were not raised to think about our mental health, or to think about our-selves at all. We labored in the shadow of the baby boomers, who were clearly never going to go away.

It is important to note that the hyperintellectualization I was taught as a child was the passport to success in my professional world, which was run almost exclusively by white men. They prized logic and reasoning over lived experience. Emotions (other than their yelling) were ignored or held in contempt. This gave me an advantage professionally because my specific trauma drove me deeper into this way of being. But it deadened my soul and kept me disconnected from myself and ultimately others. I wasn't consciously aware of this at the time. But look-ing back I can see it all very clearly.

Intellectualizing everything doesn't inspire bouts of humility or empathy. It's a type of thinking and being that is oriented toward "winning" debates and dominating people who dis-agree with you. As with "cancel culture" critics, those who in-tellectualize expect that if someone in the dominant culture causes harm, they deserve grace—they don't need to listen and change. The people complaining need to suck it up.

This is how you end up with free speech absolutists demand-ing that people from marginalized groups and their allies show grace toward people who disrespect, demonize, and even de-humanize them. The argument is essentially, "Hey, just give people space to say what they want and if you don't like it, then ignore it or go and debate them." But why should any person be forced to argue in favor of their humanity?

Why should students stay silent when their classmates invite someone to campus who has engaged in rhetoric that dehu-manizes them or their peers, and may do so when they give a speech? The "more speech is the answer to bad speech" slogan started to fall apart for me once I considered that we are telling people they are obligated to argue for their basic dignity and rights on their own campus. As a matter of law, there is no doubt that hate speech is constitutionally protected speech. But that doesn't mean there can't be social sanctions if people demean groups in an effort to "other" or disempower them.

That's not to say that there are never overzealous attacks against people who have caused upset or offense. I cited in my book the example of a female student at the University of Alaska Fairbanks who was forced to defend the student newspaper against a sexual harassment complaint. The complaint was lodged by a female professor offended by a satirical column the student wrote on April Fools' Day that said the university was planning to build a vagina-shaped building.[25] The student, who described herself as a feminist, was put through multiple investigations at the behest of the complaining professor. Or there was the University of Central Florida professor who was placed on administrative leave for making a joke in a study session equating his tough questions to a "killing spree."[26] These kinds of punitive overreactions—which happen more than you'd think—are highly problematic.

In many cases these controversies are about important issues: the dignity and rights of LGBTQIA people, racism, misogyny, and other forms of bigotry. We should not be surprised when students don't want to debate their humanity or have the humanity of other students debated. When Ben Shapiro goes on campuses and says trans people suffer from a mental disorder, why are they expected to join the debate and argue that they are, in fact, sane?[27] We should also not be surprised that there are people who will be activated by speakers who contest sexual assault statistics, because they have trauma related to this.

The truth is that—like most things—free speech is a very complicated topic with many competing factors at play. Rather than really considering this, I reflexively staked out an extremely binary view and published a whole book about it. That doesn't mean I was wrong on every count; it means I got a lot wrong, and even when I got things right, I had loads of grace for the people who were causing the upset and sometimes even harm, and little to no grace for the people who felt disrespected and victimized.

I'd still like to see students, and our culture at large, more willing to embrace debates or conversations about differing opinions among people of good faith (versus the "rhetorical dope peddlers"). I referenced in my book how Swarthmore College students tried to get a talk by renowned Princeton professors Robert George and Cornel West canceled. Known for their friendship despite their diametrically opposed worldviews, they agreed to come and speak about the importance of respectfully coexisting with people with whom you disagree. Afterward, one student complained to the student newspaper that she was "really bothered" with "the whole idea . . . that at a liberal arts college we need to be hearing a diversity of opinion."[28] It's interesting to note here that in 2019 social scientist Jonathan Haidt tweeted, "The cure for . . . confirmation bias is humility plus viewpoint diversity."[29]

Humility is hard. It requires vulnerability. Zen masters call it having a "beginner's mind."[30] Jesus tells us to approach life like little children. This means putting ourselves in a perpetual state of curiosity and wonder about the world, other people, and even ourselves. We need to be open to being surprised, chagrined, and—horror of horrors—even absolutely wrong.

On the path to grace, there is a lot working against us psychologically and culturally. But I can all but guarantee that if you choose to go this route, you will eventually come face-to-face with your own failings. God is never content to leave us where we are.

When I awoke to my self-righteous and self-certain tendencies, I was mortified. But when I shared my realization with my spiritual director, he reminded me that it was a grace to have your sin revealed to you and that I should feel encouraged by this revelation. It's called the "grace of compunction." "The Latin word *compunctio* means a piercing," the Australian monk Michael Casey wrote in *The Road to Eternal Life;* "it is like sticking a pin in somebody with the purpose of waking them up." Casey cites Saint John Cassian, who defined compunction as whatever can "by God's grace waken our lukewarm and sleepy souls." He conjured up images of us "living our spiritual lives in a slumberous state of half-wakefulness."[31] The grace of compunction nudges—or in some cases, shakes—us out of our confusion.

I realized at the end of 2020, when I read Pope Francis's book *Let Us Dream,* that I had unknowingly engaged in something called "self-accusation."[32] "Rather than accusing others for their failures and limitations, I find some fault or attitude in myself," wrote Pope Francis. Or as Jesus said, we should take the plank out of our own eye, rather than obsessing about the speck in someone else's.[33] The Pope traces this practice back to a sixth-century desert monk, Dorotheus of Gaza. To engage in it "costs nothing but our pride," writes Francis. For many of us, that is a very steep price. I won't lie: the process of approaching my past work and relationships with a fresh eye and a heap of humility was initially excruciating. But in the end, it was more than worth it.

If we want to overcome our rigid certainty, we need to get to a place where we can recognize that we may not fully understand every issue and that our brain is often working against us when we try to discern the truth of a situation or person. We would be wise to remember also that with the passage of time we often come to see things quite differently. This should cause us to show humility when confronting issues or people. This is as true in politics as it is in our personal lives.

For people who are older, we have to fight against myopia and comfort and being wedded to the way things have always been. Younger people need to open up to hearing the hard-earned wisdom of those who have gained the kind of deeper perspective that can only come from experience. There is a tension to be found here that has so far eluded us—and will only be discovered if we can approach each other with humility.

Developing intellectual humility gave grace just enough room to sneak in and help me see many things I was so sure about from a different viewpoint. As someone once said, "I once was blind, but now I see." Yes, grace is so amazing that it can help us see what is right in front of us, if only we choose to look.

Chapter 11

PATHWAYS TO REPAIR

Repentance . . . has to be based on an acknowledgment
of what was done wrong, and therefore on disclosure of the truth.
You cannot forgive what you do not know.

—DESMOND TUTU[1]

*I*ntellectual hubris makes us think we *know* more than others,
but moral superiority deludes us into believing we *are* better
than others. If this is our frame of mind, offering grace to the
no-good person or people who have offended or upset us is
essentially a nonstarter.

Social scientists have dubbed this kind of attitude "motive
attribution asymmetry." The term means we believe not only
that we are motivated by good but that the other side is motivated by bad. We are morally upright and they are rotten to the
core. In this context, there is no good-faith disagreement. Depending on which side you sit, people who oppose tax cuts on
the wealthy are motivated by selfishness, and people who support those same cuts hate rich people.

Our sense that we are uniquely good is not based on any
facts. Social scientists have kindly labeled this an "illusion of
moral superiority"—but really, it's a delusion. Why does it matter that people are deluded about their own righteousness? A

University of London study found that "most people believe they are just, virtuous, and moral . . . [which] likely contribute[s] to the severity of human conflict. When opposing sides are convinced of their own righteousness, escalation of violence is more probable, and the odds of resolution are ominously low."[2] There is no correlation between this belief and self-esteem, so it can't be chalked up to generally having a positive view of ourselves, which is a good and healthy thing.

People who believe they are inherently more moral than others say things like "I would *never* do or say the offensive thing so-and-so just did." They would *never* do the harmful act another person just did; or espouse the problematic view that another person holds. They believe they would have been the German who hid Jews, and the white person who marched against segregation in the Jim Crow South. You could put them in any context, at any point in history, and they would have always believed and done the right things. A person who holds this image of themselves cannot offer other people grace. Because they cannot comprehend their own moral frailties or the idea that they are largely the product of the family, culture, and position in society they were born into, they are quick to judge and slow to empathize.

This tendency to believe we are better than others—known as the "better than average" effect—is especially pronounced when it comes to moral qualities. So the differential will be larger if you ask a person if they are more honest than others (moral characteristic) than if you ask them if they are more competent or possess more wisdom than others (both non-moral, but desirable, characteristics).[3]

This tendency may be why when someone lies to us, we are quick to describe them as a "liar," but when we lie to another person, we find ways to justify our lie or treat it as an aberration. When we do something, it's an action that we took for external reasons; when another person does it, it is intrinsically who they are. "Most people consider themselves paragons of virtue; yet few individuals perceive this abundance of virtue in others," the authors of the University of London study wryly noted.[4]

Moral superiority isn't just for Americans. It's cross-cultural. In a study of fifty-four countries, participants ascribed the moral traits of "fairness" and "honesty" to themselves at a consistently higher rate than desirable nonmoral traits. People believe that their goodness is innate and will never change, even if they lose other nonmoral but desirable characteristics, such as intelligence or being knowledgeable, over time.[5] The high marks people give themselves on moral traits is totally irrational, since there is no reason for people to so consistently believe that they are that much different from their peers.

Overcoming the illusion of moral superiority requires you to abandon the notion that you are uniquely moral and people who don't share your beliefs can't possibly have your moral intuition and discernment. In other words: it's time to dismount the high horse.

Because we believe so strongly that we are not just inherently good but also better than others, we can be very defensive when we screw up. We can focus on our "good intentions" to try to distract from or mitigate the harm we caused. In these situations, many people call for "grace"—by which they mean "stop making such a big deal about it"—when what is actually needed is repentance and accountability.

The word *repentance* is almost completely absent from our public lexicon. Doubling down, defending, lashing out, playing the victim, screaming about "cancel culture," and making excuses all seem to have become the American way. At the other end of the spectrum, companies and celebrities seek to quell a raging Twitter mob by putting out workshopped apologies that ignore the hallmarks of true repentance. Even when the apology is sincere, people misunderstand it to mean they have engaged in the multistep process of repentance.

So, what should a pathway to repair look like? What should

we expect from people who have committed wrongs that they want to make right? Our culture offers disappointingly few clues, but the twelfth-century Jewish thinker Maimonides, who developed the steps to repentance laid out in the Talmud, provides an excellent framework for us to consider.

Rabbi Danya Ruttenberg, author of the forthcoming book *On Repentance: Repair and Amends in an Unapologetic World,* explained in an interview that in the Talmud, repentance is a multilayered process. As in Christianity, repentance must take place at the level where the harm occurred. Public acts require public repentance, for example. If the act is private, then your repentance must be directed to anyone who may have been hurt. The repentance process could take five minutes or five years, depending on the nature of the harm caused and the transformation required.

Rabbi Ruttenberg explains that when you take the first step—making a "confession articulating clearly what harm was caused"[6]—you need to own the damage you committed. This is the necessary preamble to apology. "It's an articulation of the harm you caused and a commitment to starting to do the work of changing [into] the kind of person who doesn't do the harmful thing again," Ruttenberg told me.[7] The reason you don't go directly to an apology, which is what many of us believe is the best first (and sometimes only) step, is that in order to offer a sincere apology, you should deeply reflect on the harm you caused. You need to go through the steps of repentance.

Because we live in a culture that believes the very first thing you should do when you screw up is to apologize you will probably make things worse by not including an apology up front. My recommendation would be to add an apology when you own the harm, but if you have caused serious damage, and go through all the steps of repentance, another apology will likely be the natural outflowing of that process. What I've realized is that when I take time to really consider the harm I've done, the ultimate apology I offer is more specific and heartfelt, because I have come to truly empathize with the other person.

The second step, "beginning the work of transformation," is when you start the endeavor of changing your behavior. This could be "prayer, supplication, maybe changing your location . . . [like] if you need to get out of a toxic space," Ruttenberg explained in a podcast interview with Nadia Bolz-Weber. It could be "therapy, rehab, education . . . reading books. There are all sorts of ways you can begin to try to change from the person who did that harm."[8] In today's world we might call this "doing the work."

But people can't change, right? I hear this all the time, and it has always struck me as an obviously false assertion. Yes, it's next to impossible for us to change *other* people. But for people who really want to change themselves, transformation is entirely achievable—*if* we are willing to dedicate ourselves to it.

In my case, the first step was when I acknowledged in my *USA Today* column and on Twitter the harm I felt I had caused through my participation in our poisonous public debate. I pledged to do better. "The work" began with removing myself from Twitter, which for me was a toxic space, and ending my nonstop consumption of the news, particularly opinion pieces that just reaffirmed my beliefs and stoked my outrage. I started therapy to begin examining and integrating trauma and learning how to be different. I spent time reevaluating my past work and behavior through fresh, and critical, eyes. I read books to help me unlearn my dualistic ways of thinking and to become informed about my biases, privileges, and blind spots. Those first, halting steps turned into the larger project of this book. This work has continued, and I don't know when or if it will end.

Steps two, three, and four go together. Here you are required to make amends or provide some kind of restitution and offer an apology. Again, the level of restitution depends on the level of harm you caused. "Maimonides is very, very victim-centered," says Ruttenberg. "So it's not, 'I checked it off the list, I don't know why they're still mad.' It's 'I'm attending to the person who was harmed and their needs and their feelings and their concerns.' And we're not necessarily presuming forgiveness."[9] If you do this right, the person you harmed will feel "appeased, pacified, better [and] as healed as possible." When a harm is caused, there should be deference to the person or the group who has experienced the harm.

How do you know if you have completed the repentance process? Ruttenberg says you know this when you are faced with the opportunity to repeat the misdeed but this time choose not to, because you're conscious of the harm it would do.

This book is part of my attempt at amends and restitution. It's my offering to the world to try to help shift the way we think about and treat each other, to own in more detail some of my more regrettable moments, and to apologize for them. I've also donated money to people and organizations that support the groups I harmed with my cluelessness, callousness, self-righteousness, and privilege. Where it's been appropriate, I've made direct apologies. In the end, the process of repentance likely has changed me far more than it will change any other person who reads this book, or to whom I've apologized. The fruit of this work is a changed heart and a changed woman, who not only doesn't want to repeat the harms of the past but is dedicated to creating wholeness in a fractured country.

One of the places that people tend to get tripped up in the repentance process is figuring out how to apologize. This is partly because apologizing hasn't been properly modeled in our culture, and also because when we screw up, we tend to get defensive and look for ways to minimize our wrongdoing because facing up to it is too painful. When we do this, our apologies can stir up more anger than was already there, because we really weren't apologizing. We were shifting blame and making excuses.

Getting the apology right is actually critical to the process. Apologies should be specific in that they name exactly what you did wrong. They take total responsibility and don't seek to justify the wrong through excuses or discussion of intent. A lack of bad intent may cause the harmed party to be more merciful and it is typically a factor in determining what accountability or punishment should look like, but to bring it up in the course of an apology makes it seem like the harm the other person experienced was lessened simply because you didn't intend for it to happen.

Compare and contrast these two "apologies":

Apology one: "I didn't intend to offend you with my off-color joke. I'm sorry that you got so upset."

Apology two: "It was completely indefensible to tell a joke about a woman being sexually harassed. I realize I have some work to do understanding the issues of sexism in the workplace, and I am totally committed to doing that work. I am so sorry for my behavior."

The first apology is vague. It downplays what happened and makes the person who was upset the problem. The second apology is specific, owns the behavior completely, includes vows to do better, and offers sincere regret for the offensive behavior.

Emory University philosopher George Yancy demonstrated how to apologize in a 2015 *New York Times* op-ed outlining the many ways his internalized sexism had harmed women.

"I have failed women," he wrote. "I have failed to speak out when I should have. I have failed to engage critically and extensively their pain and suffering in my writing. I have failed to transcend the rigidity of gender roles in my own life. I have failed to challenge those poisonous assumptions that women are 'inferior' to men or to speak out loudly in the company of male philosophers who believe that feminist philosophy is just a non-philosophical fad. I have been complicit with, and have allowed myself to be seduced by, a country that makes billions of dollars from sexually objectifying women, from pornography, commercials, video games, to Hollywood movies. I am not innocent."[10] He discussed his commitment to fight against his own sexism and described his efforts to use his position as a professor to help his male students identify and talk about their own sexism.

Yancy did not write this op-ed as a way to clean up a mess he had made. He wasn't in the throes of a "Me Too" accusation. He wrote it to express contrition and to model self-examination and accountability when he realized that his own biases and behaviors had blinded him to the harm he'd done.

It's rare to see someone apologize publicly when they haven't been caught doing something they shouldn't. If the most common way for people to have a "road to Damascus" moment—when their eyes are opened to the ways they have caused harm—is to have their behavior called out publicly or exposed, then how can we tell if they are sincere?

A simple answer is to look for the receipts. As outlined by Rabbi Ruttenberg, a truly repentant person will take complete responsibility and actively try to bring wholeness where they caused brokenness.

A good example of a repentance with no receipts is the "Resolution on Racial Reconciliation" that was released by the Southern Baptist Convention in June 1995.[11] In this resolution, the convention—which represents the largest Protestant denomination in the United States—apologized for its role in supporting slavery and opposing the civil rights of African Americans. (The Southern Baptist Convention was formed in 1845 over disagreements about slavery with Northern Baptists.) Their 1995 resolution used the word *repent,* but the statement was really just an apology. They acknowledged that "we continue to reap a bitter harvest" from slavery, adding that "the racism which yet plagues our culture today is inextricably tied to the past." But there was nothing said about making amends or offering restitution, both of which should be the natural fruit of true repentance. (The Southern Baptist theology of repentance oddly does not require amends or restitution.[12])

In essence, the Southern Baptist Convention belatedly got it half right—arguably the easy half: they acknowledged their role in the original harm committed by this country. What they've yet to do is take the meaningful next steps down the pathway to repair. If the largest Christian denomination in America thinks an apology is repentance, then we shouldn't be surprised that the average American makes the same mistake.

In 2021, following release of the documentary *Framing Britney Spears,* Justin Timberlake came under attack for the way he had contributed to the misogynistic treatment of Spears and the misogyny and racism directed at Janet Jackson. He eventually posted an apology for not appreciating the preferential treatment he received as a white male performer.[13]

The apology seemed sincere, if vague. If Timberlake has truly had his eyes opened to the reality of misogyny and racism in the business that has served him so well, there are many actions he could take as a man of enormous means and influence. He could start an organization dedicated to supporting female and BIPOC artists, for example. He could regularly speak out when he sees misogyny and racism in the industry. Hopefully we will see Timberlake taking these kinds of steps in the future.

Contrition at gunpoint is too often our culture's norm, but there is another way to do things. If you become aware that you have caused harm, you should consider "telling on yourself." Confess and go through the steps of repentance because you are sincerely sorry, not because you have been caught by someone else.

I've seen this process in practice. A number of years back, someone took a chance by coming to me to ask for forgiveness. He had been senior to me in one of my past jobs and wouldn't take no for an answer when he asked me out for a date. He kept calling and emailing me and sending me flowers. I ended up quitting since reporting the behavior would've made future employment difficult, if not impossible.

A year later, this man reached out to me. He didn't ask for forgiveness because he was worried about getting in trouble—this was twenty years ago, when men tended not to get in trouble for such things. His apology was heartfelt and specific. Rather than stopping at "I'm sorry," he named everything he had done wrong. He told me he had gone to a therapist to get help with his anger after I'd rebuffed him and he retaliated.

I forgave him, and while we aren't friends today, I have no ill will toward him.

When people "tell on themselves," the consequences are typically not as harsh as if they wait to be exposed or confronted. Most parents will respond more mercifully if their teenager comes to them and confesses to doing something wrong than if they discover the bad behavior the teenager has failed to disclose, or even worked to hide.

Sincere remorse has the power to unleash grace.

I personally experienced grace when I acknowledged how I had gotten something wrong in a very public way.

When I started attending an evangelical church in 2005, I wanted to do the right thing in adapting to my new faith. In my twenties and early thirties I had marched in the streets in support of abortion rights and viewed any person who didn't share my support as an inveterate misogynist. But following my religious conversion, I found myself surrounded by Christians with a vastly different perspective on the issue.

While I didn't support making abortion illegal, I latched onto the one area where I could find common cause with my fellow white evangelical Christians: an opposition to abortions late in pregnancy. I penned some columns on the subject that I now deeply regret. The unspoken premise of these writings was that women were going through the trouble of carrying a pregnancy for seven or eight months and then capriciously deciding to end it. What I know now—and would have known then if I had shown a little humility—is that there are all sorts of reasons why women make the decision to end pregnancies later in the term. Most often, the reason is a threat to their health or the fact that the fetus is not viable.

Throughout 2017 and 2018, as my icy self-certainty about this issue thawed under the gaze of grace, the overly binary positions I had staked out concerning abortion caused me great consternation. When I reread my past columns with new eyes, it was hard to believe that I was the one who wrote them. They weren't very well reasoned and assumed such bad faith on the part of so many people. I felt real regret but wasn't sure what to do about it. Then, in 2019, in the face of increasing threats by Republicans to roll back abortion rights through so-called fetal heartbeat laws, more and more women had begun to share stories[14] about their own abortions later in pregnancy.[15] As I read these stories, I felt ill thinking of the pain my past writing may have caused women in these extremely difficult situations.

I wanted to apologize and express my evolution in a column, but frankly I was scared. I didn't know how to explain why I had gotten it so wrong. If I didn't understand my reasoning, how would anyone else? Still, I finally screwed up the courage to express my regrets regarding my earlier columns.

I took a deep breath and laid it all out: "I wish I could press 'delete' on some of my past columns. I was particularly vicious toward Planned Parenthood, despite my long support for the work they do to increase health care access for women. When it came to abortion later in pregnancy, I employed my now signature black-and-white thinking on a complicated topic that required more care." After I became an evangelical, I wrote, "I was surrounded by people who believed that one could not be a 'real Christian' if they weren't 'pro-life.'" "I wanted to be a real Christian." I explained that I was new to faith, and I trusted that the people around me understood the Bible better than I did, even if I could not find a single reference to abortion in the entire book.[16]

Then I addressed the elephant in the room: "Am I still a 'pro-life' Christian?" I asked. Leaning into a little nonbinary thinking, I declared my faith "as strong as ever" and called myself "both pro-choice and pro-life." While I always believed I wouldn't have gotten an abortion had I faced an unplanned pregnancy, I had realized there really was no way to know that for sure. "I know enough women who swore they were anti-abortion all the way up to the point when they saw the plus sign on that little white stick to know it's pure hubris to say with certainty what decision I would have made," I wrote.

As I reflect back on it now, I realize I am actually just pro-choice. I believe abortion should be legal, and that's what "pro-choice" means. The term "pro-life," on the other hand, is not really about supporting life, because if it was, people who identify with that label would support universal health care, speak out against police killing unarmed citizens, and oppose the death penalty. I realize there are people who identify as pro-life who *do* hold all of those views, but that is not what the pro-life movement is about. The pro-life movement is about ending abortion rights, full stop.

As my editor prepared the column for publication, I had a pit in my stomach. I deserved whatever was coming from the women I had demonized. I was also ready to be ostracized by Christians who I knew would lecture me about how I wasn't a "real" Christian and warn against my impending trip to Hell.

Then something totally unexpected happened.

That something was grace.

No, it wasn't from the professional Christians. It was from feminist abortion rights supporters. Instead of raking me over the coals for my past behavior, they expressed appreciation for my reconsideration of my past views.

At the same time, I heard from everyday Christians who identified with my argument, having taken their own journeys to a similar conclusion. I heard privately from leading Christian figures who thanked me for taking an important step in shifting how Christians can think about this issue. It didn't mean hectoring tweets weren't rolling in from the self-appointed enforcers of Christian doctrine, or that stories about me "misleading" Christians or pushing "misinformation" weren't being written. Of course that happened too.

But rather than firing off angry or defensive tweets to these responses, I chose to view them through the lens of grace. I didn't judge the authors or demonize them the way they were doing to me, because I was now able to recognize the self-righteousness and knew all too well the insidious pull of binary thinking.

One of the reasons people can be resistant to the idea of grace is that they've seen the idea—or ancillary concepts like unity and healing—used to avoid accountability. This is because it's difficult to have healing without repentance and accountability when a great harm has occurred.

After Trump supporters stormed the Capitol and left five dead, Republican leaders tried to sweep everything under the rug, making hollow calls for "unity" even though they had enabled the president in his demonstrably false claims that the election had been stolen. They didn't bother to apologize or take responsibility, let alone engage in acts of repentance. They argued for "healing" rather than holding President Trump responsible for inciting the mob, which even a few Republican leaders had acknowledged he had done. To date, not one Re-

publican elected official has actually taken responsibility for
their role in that attack, nor has any Republican leader been
held accountable.[17]

When a parent has abused or neglected their child and the
government removes that child for their safety, the parent
doesn't get to say, "Let me have my child back so we can start
healing." The parent has to essentially go through the steps of
repentance. They must confess to what they've done wrong.
They have to demonstrate that they have done the work to
change, through rehabilitation or whatever else is necessary.
The parent has to earn the privilege of being with their child
again. They will have to apologize for their behavior and promise not to cause the harm again. They will have to consistently
interact with their child in supervised conditions in a way that
demonstrates that they have changed. There will be strict
boundaries around their interactions with their child unless and
until the parent has demonstrated that they are safe. That's the
law. It's also common sense.

Grace does not bypass accountability. Grace without repentance and accountability is called "enabling." Grace creates the
space for repentance, repair, and reconciliation. It means we
don't judge or label the person who has done wrong as irre-
deemable and beyond hope. But it doesn't mean we just move
on like nothing happened if real harm has occurred.

We need to create a culture of repentance in which people
take responsibility for their actions and labor to create wholeness where they've caused brokenness. One way to encourage
this kind of behavior is to normalize the idea that people who
have made mistakes deserve another chance, and to be willing
to welcome them back with open arms when they have made
things right, because we've made our focus restoring and transforming our culture, not seeking retribution.

Chapter 12

EMBRACE HEALTHY CONFLICT

Fight for the things you care about, but do it in a way
that will lead others to join you.

—Ruth Bader Ginsburg[1]

Perhaps one of the greatest misconceptions about grace is that it means being passive, or not standing up for your beliefs or not confronting people about problematic or harmful behavior. The image too many people have of a "graceful" person is of someone who just lets others do and say whatever they want and eschews the idea of accountability. They envision a person who doesn't get angry and who, rather than speaking up about behavior that is causing harm, suffers quietly or allows others to suffer. When an argument breaks out, we think the person who tries to persuade everyone to just "get along" and not disrupt the peace is working to achieve grace. An appeaser, in other words. A doormat.

But grace is not about inaction or holding your tongue when you have something to say that might upset other people. It's not a magic wand to make discord disappear. Discord is part of life—and the great religious traditions treat it as such. "Jesus' teachings take conflict for granted," theologian Barbara Brown

Taylor has written. "You can't love an enemy if you don't have one. You can't turn *this* cheek if no one slaps *that* one first."[2] What Jesus taught was how to handle that conflict.

Healthy conflict is what I think Jesus is talking about when in the Sermon on the Mount, he tells the crowd, "Blessed are the peacemakers."[3] Note a crucial omission: he makes no mention of peace*keepers,* those who maintain peace by avoiding or suppressing conflict. A peacemaker, on the other hand, works to get to the heart of whatever is causing division, and labors to create wholeness that does not paper over differences or bypass the need for repentance or accountability if that's what is called for. Peacekeepers just want the conflict to disappear, usually because it's in their best interest for that to happen.

Because many of us didn't grow up in families where healthy conflict was modeled, and because our public figures often behave in such a toxic manner, a lot of us don't know what healthy conflict looks like. When engaged in properly, conflict is an act of peace*making.* When a couple is married and they have healthy conflict, their conversations help them understand each other better, and each new conflict creates more intimacy. It brings them closer to each other, not farther apart. Even if the couple doesn't see eye to eye on everything, their conflict leads to a better marriage.

By contrast, couples who engage in peace*keeping* by ignoring their problems will find themselves drifting away from each other as they develop resentment and worse. Then there are couples who engage in conflict but do it in such an unhealthy manner that it leaves one or both parties feeling emotionally battered and bruised. Each time this happens, they grow farther apart.

Sometimes the fractures from those unhealthy conflicts become so great that the marriage collapses. So it is with countries, where endless unhealthy conflicts devolve into utter chaos and even civil war.

That may seem hyperbolic, but it's a sentiment I hear often from people who have engaged in peace and reconciliation work in other countries. An expert on the subject, Tihomir Kukolja, told me in late 2020 that what was happening in the United States reminded him of Yugoslavia in the years leading up to the war that broke out there in the 1990s. And that was months before President Trump and other Republican leaders incited a mob to storm the U.S. Capitol in an effort to overturn the election.

"As we were headed for war, the main issue was a sense of growing division," Kukolja told me. "Communities were divided. I remember the two years leading to war and we thought, *No, it's not going to happen and a solution is going to be found.* But looking back now, I can see everything was heading towards war."

Kukolja noted that during this period, hate language in the former Yugoslavia was intensifying until vitriol engulfed the national discourse. "All sides were demonizing, degrading, and dehumanizing each other," he told me. "Serbian and Croatian radio and TV media played a major role in inciting people to war. They often manufactured and exaggerated various incidents to make people angry and willing to fight."[4]

Imagine how much worse this might have been had the Internet existed, as it does today. Kukolja told me that it was only in the wreckage of the country that its war-weary citizens expressed a reluctant openness to coexisting without demonizing and dehumanizing one another.

Perhaps the United States could avoid the same "destroy the village in order to save it" path.

This doesn't mean we need to give up our differences. We are not all the same, and we will never all see the world the same way. Nor do we need to coddle other people to make them feel better about their bad behavior or problematic beliefs. Sometimes people will claim you are not offering them grace when you criticize them or say things they don't want to hear. Conservatives frequently tell me I am being divisive when I talk about racism or misogyny. But naming issues and problems is not divisive and is not anti-grace. We need to call a thing a thing, as they say.

Once we are clear about what we need to say, we have to take time to get clear about *how* to say it and *why* we are saying it. Having uncomfortable and hard conversations is the path to personal growth and societal change. However, the way to make these conversations happen isn't so straightforward.

"The Book of Ephesians tells us to speak truth in love," the historian and *New York Times* bestselling author Jemar Tisby told me in an interview. "I think that's a component of grace as well—that we are truth-tellers. Not to tear people down, but to build them up. The point is wholeness and restoration and flourishing."[5]

Tisby, the author of *How to Fight Racism* and *The Color of Compromise,* suggests we ask ourselves a simple question: "What is my motivation for speaking truth? Am I using truth as a sledgehammer to destroy or a scalpel to heal? Fannie Lou Hamer said 'Ain't no such a thing as I can hate anybody and hope to see God's face.' Or the way Martin Luther King Jr. put it, 'We are caught in an inescapable network of mutuality, tied in a single garment of destiny. Whatever affects one directly, affects all indirectly.' These Christian activists spoke truth all the time but with this idea that my flourishing is wrapped up in yours. I'm speaking truth so that you can act better, but I'm also speaking it because I know that your healing is connected to my healing as well. That's just something we tend to lose in the public discourse."[6]

How often can we say this is how we approach conflict or serious disagreement? When offended and outraged, many of us are much more likely to turn to the kind of demonization and self-righteous lecturing that drives disconnection. Viewing ourselves as bound up in mutuality with someone who is saying upsetting things or even causing harm can feel like a bridge too far.

For our purposes, let's just call this person your father. Your dad loves how Donald Trump "owns the libs" and thinks that Kamala Harris is the Antichrist. (Don't even bother reminding him that he used the same label for Bill Clinton, then Hillary Clinton, then Barack Obama.) You text your dad a *Washington Post* article detailing Trump's many lies. You remind him that lying is a sin and that Trump is a racial demagogue who puts kids in cages. But your dad gets all his information from Fox News, and host Laura Ingraham told him that those children were being treated like they were at summer camp. Your dad believes the "liberal media" hates Trump and will say anything to discredit him. This is just another example of their mendacious lies, he tells you. You don't really expect your dad to believe you more than Laura Ingraham, do you? Because he knows where you get your information: *fake news*.

Also, he may or may not say this, but your father has noticed that ever since you moved to New York, or Washington, DC, or Seattle or wherever else your new liberal enclave happens to be, you've changed. You think you are better than he is. You are just like all those fancy-pants lefty elitists that Sean Hannity was talking about on the radio this afternoon. You've been brainwashed by the "woke mob."

I urge you: take a breath. Rather than assaulting your father with a litany of facts, with a dose of contempt and condescension thrown in, take a second to see if you can get in the mindset of grace. Pull the lens back and look at the bigger picture.

If you view your father through the prism of grace, a few things happen. First, you see him as a whole person. He is *both* a person who is saying very upsetting things *and* the person who sat and cheered for you at every Little League game or wiped away your tears when your first love broke up with you.

Grace helps you see him as more than his deeply troubling political views.

Second, you don't need to demonize him, either verbally or in your head, because you can use boundaries instead. You recognize your father's beliefs belong to him and not you. This is the point where you decide whether you have the capacity to engage with him—and whether he has the capacity to receive what you have to say—or if you want to shut the conversation down. Should you choose to move forward with your conversation, you should set boundaries around how it will take place.

Sometimes, the path of least resistance is to walk away and preserve your sanity. If your father is driving you nuts because he's always telling you how to raise your children, that's a very different kind of disagreement than him expressing racist, misogynist, or homophobic views, for example. In the former case, I'd suggest telling him you don't want to discuss it with him and leaving it at that. He doesn't have a say in the issue, unless you ask him for advice. In the latter case, I'd try engaging him using the tools of healthy conflict.

When people are being systemically harmed, though, we should try to be peacemakers, which almost always means engaging in some difficult conversations. The "Beloved Community" as Rev. Dr. Martin Luther King Jr. envisioned it is not just one where people love and care for each other; it is a community rooted in equality and justice for all people. We all have a responsibility to speak up when those values are being violated if we think we can make a difference.

Embracing healthy conflict is part of what it means to be an ally. If you are a white person and you don't talk to your family about the racist views they express, then guess who really suffers? It's not you. Black and Indigenous people, and people of color, are the ones who pay the price for your family member's racist beliefs in myriad and uncountable ways. The same goes for pretty much every issue where people are being marginalized and harmed. It's why Christian author Jen Hatmaker told her LGBTQIA fans that she would do the work of bridge building and talking with people who don't support LGBTQIA rights, so that they didn't have to.

I will add a caveat: you are never obligated to have a conversation that puts you in emotional or physical jeopardy. Just make sure you aren't confusing safety with comfort. Be honest with yourself: Are you avoiding conflict because it makes you feel uncomfortable? Or are you declining to engage because you know the person is incapable of receiving feedback or will become verbally or physically abusive if you confront them? Are you staying quiet when someone says something bigoted because you'd rather just watch Netflix than have an uncomfortable conversation, or are you avoiding confrontation because you are struggling with depression and you know you lack the emotional capacity for additional stress at this moment?

Journalist Amanda Ripley, author of the 2021 book *High Conflict: Why We Get Trapped and How We Get Out,* makes a distinction between healthy conflict and what she calls "high conflict." "With good conflict, you can still get really angry and frustrated—it can be intense and heated—but there's a feeling that it's going somewhere . . . people tend to leave the conflict more satisfied, even if they don't agree," Ripley explained in a 2021 interview.[7] "High conflict can start small, but it becomes an us-vs.-them kind of feud," she notes. "It becomes all-consuming and takes on a life of its own. There is a feeling of being stuck in high conflict, being frozen, and you just have the same fights over and over."

Unfortunately, Ripley confirms what most of us have experienced at one time or another: "There are people who want to have high conflict. They're getting a lot out of it—maybe a sense of power . . . maybe meaning. Especially when there's a power difference, that's a problem you can't fix sometimes."[8] In such a case, the best way for you to respond to behavior and beliefs that you are a "no" to is to turn your focus onto your "yes." Use your energy to volunteer or donate money, rather than throwing your pearls before swine.

Should you decide to try to open up a conversation with the hope of trying to get someone to see an issue differently, remember that changing people's minds about their beliefs is very hard—and if it does happen, it probably won't be overnight. Rome was not built in a day, but we do know that people *can* change their minds, including about controversial issues, over time.

Americans' views on a range of topics have changed significantly in my lifetime. Seventy percent of Americans support same-sex marriage today.[9] In 2009 that number was 40 percent; in 1996 only 27 percent of Americans held that view. Almost every person I know who reassessed their beliefs on the topic did so because of having a relationship with LGBTQIA people or seeing their relationships represented accurately in the media. It wasn't because people were calling them "homophobes" or bombarding them with facts. I know, because throughout my twenties that's exactly what I did, and it never worked.

This points toward a wider truth: What changes people's minds, it turns out, are usually not facts or shaming but the sharing of personal stories. Grace, it so happens, plays a key role here.

A study by political scientists published in 2020 found that nonjudgmentally exchanging personal stories can lead to durable changes in people's exclusionary (prejudiced) beliefs.[10] "Advocates often call out unacceptable views, which can intensify people's resistance, or they make their case through talking points and related facts, which our work shows has little effect," Joshua Kalla, one of the authors of the study, told *Yale News*. "We found that simply listening and sharing a relevant personal story successfully lessened people's resistance and increased their openness to change."[11]

The authors conducted three field experiments where canvassers went door to door and used a respectful, conversational approach to try to change people's attitudes about either undocumented immigrants or transgender people. Canvassers committed to listening nonjudgmentally to voters' views and sharing stories about unauthorized immigrants or transgender people, rather than engaging in traditional political canvassing, where voters are given a list of reasons to support a candidate or initiative. When they followed up with voters, the political scientists found reductions in prejudice toward both groups.

Another study published in early 2021 suggested that in order to increase your chances of being heard by a political opponent, you have to convince them that you are rational, because both sides of the spectrum are inclined to view their opponents as brainwashed and irrational.[12] "The key to fostering respect is to support your political beliefs with personal experiences, especially those involving harm," Kurt Gray, a psychology and neuroscience professor, and one of the authors of the study, explained in *USA Today*. "If you are pro-gun rights, talk less about the statistics of responsible gun ownership, and more about how you used a gun to protect your family. If you are pro-immigration, talk less about the economic potential of the DREAMers, and more about how your family was torn apart by deportation."[13]

Using facts will not solve this problem, because if someone has a strongly formed ideological or political view that happens to be contradicted by a particular fact, they are more likely to dismiss your data point than to reconsider their belief. The conversation will devolve into a disagreement about the reliability of your sources. However, opponents will view a personal experience as more rational and trustworthy.

Dave Fleischer, an organizer from the Los Angeles LGBT Center Leadership LAB, has deployed a similar technique, sometimes called "deep canvassing," with success. He told the news website *Vox* that sharing stories and allowing people to come to the conclusion on their own is much better than when someone "bitch-slaps you with a statistic."[14]

Activist Vivian Topping joined in a deep canvassing effort in Massachusetts in 2018, at a time when voters were choosing whether to keep a Massachusetts law that protected transgender rights. Topping—who identifies as nonbinary—told *Vox,* "I came out two years ago now, and one of the hardest things for me has been talking with folks who don't understand [gender identity], and not immediately writing someone off because they don't immediately get it."[15]

Topping views this as "giving them grace," which they told *Vox* "means being able to hear someone say something that can be hurtful and trying to think about how to have a real conversation and connect with them." Their work paid off when voters ultimately chose to preserve trans rights, and Topping attributes some of that success to the deep canvassing technique—which involves beginning a conversation and listening without judgment—noting that "without it we wouldn't have been able to win."[16]

If this method could work between complete strangers, it seems that it could work among people who know each other, including family. But, as I indicated in Chapter 9, with family there are even more complicated emotions at play. It's critical that clear boundaries be set if you decide to engage in healthy conflict with a family member. It's also important to remember that you are not required to put yourself in a situation in which you feel denigrated for any reason. Deep canvassing is only for people who feel drawn to engaging in this kind of exchange.

This doesn't mean that if you use a personal story you will

automatically change another person's opinion on an issue. We've all encountered people who are not affected by hearing about another person's lived experience. The point here is that in our "post-fact" world, your chances in most situations of helping a person see a different point of view are going to be greater if you share a personal story rather than blasting someone with factoids.

Even after hearing about studies lauding the impact of sharing personal experiences, this approach still seems counterintuitive, because we like to believe that we make all our decisions based on facts. "Both liberals and conservatives believe that using facts in political discussions helps to foster mutual respect, but 15 studies—across multiple methodologies and issues—show that these beliefs are mistaken," as the early 2021 study mentioned earlier found.[17] "Political opponents respect moral beliefs more when they are supported by personal experiences, not facts." The authors went on to say, "Studies show that people believe in the truth of both facts and personal experiences in nonmoral disagreement; however, in moral disagreements, subjective experiences seem truer (i.e., are doubted less) than objective facts."

Author and theologian Brian McLaren points out that many of Jesus's teachings, also called "parables," utilize story instead of facts. In doing so, he helped people detach from their typical ways of seeing things. "When you aggressively attack people's familiar ideas, they tend to respond defensively. They dig in their heels and become even more firmly attached to the very ideas that they need to be liberated from," McLaren writes.[18] "That's why Jesus, like other effective communicators, constantly told stories, stories that grabbed people by the imagination and transported them into another imaginative world."

Telling stories and sharing personal experiences is a way to sneak past people's emotional walls. Jesus "didn't spend a lot of time repeating or refuting the false statements of his critics, and he didn't counterpunch when he was attacked or insulted," McLaren notes. "Instead, he used every criticism as an opportunity to restate, clarify, and illustrate his true statements. He had, to use a contemporary phrase, *message discipline,* which drew people to his central, simple message: an invitation to overcome long-held biases, to think again, and to see and live life in a new light."[19]

In addition to avoiding overwhelming people with facts, remember to use empathy. Try to find common ground where you can. Rather than being defensive, admit when you realize you got something wrong or are not communicating in a healthy manner. All this builds trust. When your mom says something that you feel you should confront, rather than putting her down or coming at her aggressively, try calling her in and up. You might say something like "Mom, I know you are kind and loving, so when I hear you say things like that about undocumented immigrants, I experience you as being different from the mom I grew up with."

In order to engage in healthy conflict, we have to give up our judgments and beliefs about the other side, if only for the moment. If you are talking to your parents, for example, imagine how you would feel if your child (or maybe niece or nephew) grew up to embrace a political party or ideology that stood against everything you believed, and then they came home to lecture you about your stupid, immoral beliefs. You'd probably wonder where you went wrong. None of this means you should hide your views, but if you understand where other people are coming from, their reactions won't feel as threatening or confusing.

You should also do an inventory of your go-to tactics in a debate or disagreement. You might find that you engage in behavior that is unhelpful and maybe even unnecessarily antagonizing, and it needs to be changed. When Robert and I had our first fight, six years ago, he accused me of being "prosecuto-rial." A younger version of me would have denied this, but I had to admit I had heard it before. The truth is, I tend to learn through the Socratic method, so I ask a million questions in an effort to understand things more clearly. I've learned over the years that this approach can feel overly aggressive to others. I think I'm just having a debate or discussion, but the other person feels like they are on trial. We all have these kinds of blind spots that we have to work to correct.

In an essay on how to disagree, writer Paul Graham offers a helpful guide that if everyone debating politics, religion, and the like followed, we might actually be able to move past the pointless, frustrating, and rage-inducing arguments we often experience or witness online or in the media.[20] Going from lowest forms of disagreeing to highest forms, he lists the four tactics that drive me (and probably you) completely bonkers: name calling; ad hominem attacks (attacks characteristics of writer but not substance of argument); responds to tone but not the actual argument; and contradiction, which is stating "the opposing case with little or no supporting evidence."

Graham then moves to the higher forms: counterargument (contradicts and then backs up with reasoning and evidence) and refutation (finds the mistake and explains why it's wrong, ideally using quotes). Finally, he shares the crème de la crème of argumentation: explicitly refute the central point the other person has made. When engaging in healthy conflict you should try to stay in the zone of counterargument, refutation, and focusing on the central argument. The point of healthy conflict is not to "win." It's to build understanding.

Showing curiosity is another way to make people feel seen and heard and can prevent escalations. Don't assume you know what another person's motivations are. "You are just saying this because it's good for your business" would be such an accusation. Or "You only believe this because it's what your husband believes." The person is standing right in front of you. Why not just ask them how they came to have this belief? Similarly, you shouldn't tell people how they feel about things. "You don't care how much your beliefs hurt me" is a declarative statement you should avoid making unless they've actually told you they don't care about you feeling hurt.

Name-calling, labeling, and shaming are also off-limits. Shame makes people hide things; it doesn't transform them. Make sure you understand the difference between shame and guilt. As Brené Brown points out, shame is "I am bad," guilt is "I did something bad."[21] Shame sends people into self-protection mode and makes them feel like they are incapable of change; guilt, when it's healthy, can motivate people to change and helps shape our moral conscience.

My friend Amanda Hite, who grew up gay in a conservative evangelical family, shared an experience that illustrates how powerful personal stories and grace can be in changing minds. When she was home for Thanksgiving a few years ago, her uncle included in his blessing of the meal a request that God protect America from the "homosexual agenda." Amanda chose not to confront him—or share the choice words I certainly would have had for him.

Even today, as I recount this story, I feel fury building in my body as I think of my precious friend, or any LGBTQIA person, having to hear something like this. Many of us would have shamed the uncle without a second thought. Amanda, on the other hand, typically plays the long game. She wants to change people's minds, not alienate them and drive them deeper into their harmful beliefs, which is usually what happens when you shame people. She also didn't want to let him hijack her holiday.

A few years later, she brought home Julie, the woman she would end up marrying. Her uncle was smitten by Julie's warmth and wit, and by the love that Amanda and Julie had for each other. By the time they got married, two years after that upsetting Thanksgiving dinner, his opposition to the concept of same-sex relationships had melted in the face of the real relationship in front of him. He was so thrilled for Amanda and Julie that he posted a note from him and his wife on their wedding website telling them that they were the perfect couple and had shown him what Jesus's love looks like.

Amanda could have dressed her uncle down and bombarded him with facts about why his view was wrong. She would have been absolutely justified in doing so. Instead, she had clear boundaries and stayed true to her convictions about how she wanted to interact with other people, regardless of their behavior. She told me, "I always tried to model the unconditional love I hoped they'd give, and modeled kindness. I went out of my way to share stories and experiences different from what my family had heard." When I asked where she got the idea to do this, she said, "I plagiarized that from the Jesus guy in the Bible," noting that her family initially began with just tolerating her relationship with Julie and were later surprised by how it changed them.

Not every serious conflict will have a happy ending. But Amanda's story is a good reminder that people sometimes have a greater capacity to learn and change than we might expect, if we can grant them the space in which to do so.

CONCLUSION

Out beyond ideas of wrongdoing and rightdoing,
there is a field. I'll meet you there.
When the soul lies down in that grass,
the world is too full to talk about.
Ideas, language, even the phrase *each other*
doesn't make any sense.

—JALĀL AD-DĪN MUHAMMAD RŪMĪ[1]

There is no question that we are in the midst of a critical period in American history.

It can at times feel apocalyptic no matter where you are on the ideological spectrum. This instinct is more on target than many realize. When we think of an *apocalypse,* we imagine complete and total destruction. But in the original Greek, the word simply means "an uncovering or revealing." By that standard, it would be correct to call this an apocalyptic era.

It's as though America has been viewed under a magnifying glass. We are noticing fractures in our country, but that doesn't mean those fractures weren't always there. We are seeing America as it truly is, and as painful as that may be for some people, it's always better to deal with the truth than to seek comfort in a fiction.

The country elected a white nationalist demagogue who trafficked in misogyny and bigotry, who lied pathologically and demonized and bullied anyone who challenged him. He lost reelection, but only narrowly, and made false accusations about a stolen election. He incited a violent attack on the U.S. Capitol by our fellow Americans to stop certification of the election. After all that, his supporters remain legion. Before 2016, this scenario would have been unfathomable to almost everyone.

Both the election and the defeat of Donald Trump revealed so much about our country.

Because of social media, we are finally reckoning with racism, sexism, and other forms of bigotry on what feels like a near-daily basis. We are seeing and hearing people say things in public that they only used to say to friends and family. The thoughts aren't what's new; the ability to share them far and wide through social media is what has changed things.

The cruel reality of police brutality against Black people is now there for everyone to see, thanks to the technology of cellphone video. But the behavior itself is not new. No Black person was surprised by these visual revelations. This has always been their grim reality. But now it has been uncovered and disseminated in a way that cannot be ignored or denied. It's profoundly problematic that unless a video can be produced, many white people still question Black people's ability to accurately describe their life experience. It shouldn't take a video for justice to be served.

We've also had an uncovering of the long-standing harassment, abuse, and violence against women, at times perpetrated by some of society's most powerful men, and the unimaginable has occurred: many of these men have lost their jobs and reputations for their behavior. We are slowly experiencing correctives to the nation's whitewashed narrative that erases the central role the genocide of Indigenous people and kidnapping, torture, and enslavement of Black people played in the establishment of and economic dominance of the United States. Reckoning with these facts, and laboring to create wholeness where destruction occurred, should be our central task for years to come.

More and more will be revealed. Somehow, we have to learn to live with this reality and coexist with people who—and I mean this in the most "graceful" way possible—we may at times want to strangle with our bare hands.

In his influential book *Jesus and the Disinherited*, theologian Howard Thurman, a mentor of Rev. Dr. Martin Luther King Jr., wrote that Jesus's teachings were "focused on the urgency of a radical change in the inner attitude of the people." Jesus "placed his finger on the 'inward center' as the crucial arena where the issues would determine the destiny of his people." Jesus, Thurman wrote, "recognized with authentic realism that anyone who permits another to determine the quality of his inner life gives into the hands of the other the keys to his destiny."[2]

Grace is good for the world, but it's also really, really good for you.

It keeps you from giving away your power or becoming that which you oppose. When you reject the revenge, aggression, domination, and retaliation that are the hallmarks of our culture and respond with grace, you bring peace into the world. You bring peace into your heart. I hope you can see by now that grace is "thick," to borrow a formulation from Yale theologian Dr. Willie James Jennings. It is substantial and muscular. It is a force in its own right. It is our strength in times of trouble. It points us to the possibilities in people and in our country. It conjures up images of something more than what we have—of a place where the idea of the "other" does not exist.

Grace is an idea worth saving, and in the end, it might just be what saves us—in ways we have not yet imagined.

ACKNOWLEDGMENTS

Saving Grace would likely not exist had it not been for my agent at Creative Artists Agency (CAA), David Larabell, who read my *USA Today* column about wanting to bring more grace into culture and said, "That needs to be a book!" It was the determination of CAA's Rachel Adler, now my agent for television, who tracked me down and got me to answer an email (not an easy feat) encouraging me to talk to David about his idea. I'm grateful to be connected to two of the most talented agents in the business, who happen to also be wonderful humans. A special shout out to Kelly Rafferty at CAA for all her help over the past few years.

David, along with my brilliant friend Sara Corbett, helped me shape the book proposal and encouraged me to keep going when I felt it was too hefty of a topic to tackle. Through David's guidance I found the perfect partner for this project in the form of Convergent Books, where I've been blessed to work with an incredible editor, Derek Reed. Derek brought wisdom and patience in equal measure and helped me think through this difficult topic. The team at Convergent and Random House has been stellar and a delight to work with. I'm grateful to Mary Reynics, who stepped in to shepherd the book to completion when Derek went on paternity leave, along with other members of the team, including Tina Constable, Jessalyn Foggy, Lindsey Kennedy, Alisse Goldsmith-Wissman, Ashley Hong, Jessica Bright, Cindy Berman, and Sarah Horgan.

I'm lucky to have had so many incredible people agree to read chapters, and in some cases the entire manuscript, and provide feedback and perspective. I'm eternally grateful to Lisa Sharon Harper, Jonathan Merritt, Sue Dominus, Brian McLaren, Jamal Simmons, Julie Rodgers, Michelle Dubois, Miles Adcox, Shawna Watley, Pete Wehner, Athena Perrakis, Austin Houghtaling, Misha Lewis, Amanda Hite, John Draper, Heather Stephenson, and Kevin Vallier for taking time out of their busy schedules to help me.

Courtney Leak served as the unofficial therapist for this project, offering unparalleled wisdom about how trauma and the general unwellness of our society contribute to our resistance to embracing an idea like grace. She provided invaluable feedback on the manuscript, and this book would not be what it is without her. Courtney began as a source, and once I was done reporting the book, recognizing her unique skills, I asked her to be my therapist. She has served as a wise adviser, helping me find my way through my own complicated nest of unresolved issues as I fought to finish a book that felt too risky and scary to put into the world.

Angela Scheff has the most appropriate name of anyone I know. I'm convinced she is a bona fide angel, and nobody can disabuse me of this notion. She came highly recommended to me by other writers who thought she could help me when I reached that point that many writers know—where in the middle of the process you decide the book is a stupid idea. Like a mad scientist, one day I tore the manuscript apart, moving chapters and sections in a frenzy of frustration. By the time I was done, I could see no way to reassemble it. Angela helped get me back on track and became an invaluable sounding board, editor, and partner in the process of creating this book.

I also want to give a special thanks to my CNN family for the support they have shown me over the years, especially Jeff Zucker and Rebecca Kutler, who are the kinds of bosses everyone should be so fortunate to have. I feel lucky to get to work with such talented and kind colleagues. I'm grateful also to my editor at *USA Today,* David Mastio, who nearly a decade ago gave me the opportunity to write as a regular columnist at the paper and is endlessly supportive of my ideas and writing.

Last, and certainly not least, is my fiancé, Robert Draper. He was with me every step of the way, offering insight and expert writing advice, cheering me on when it felt too hard, talking through concepts and ideas, and as always, being the ultimate Dog Dad to our beloved fur children Lucy and Bill (who, for the record, were total layabouts through the whole process).

I could not have done this book without this incredible support network. It truly took a village. Thank you to one and all.

NOTES

1. The Thickness of Grace

1. Philip Yancey, *What's So Amazing About Grace?* (Grand Rapids: Zondervan, 2008).
2. Luke 15:11–32.
3. Dorothee Sölle, *The Silent Cry: Mysticism and Resistance,* trans. Barbara and Martin Rumscheldt (Minneapolis: Fortress Press, 2001), 293.
4. Mark 12:31 CEV.
5. "The Powerful Lesson Maya Angelou Taught Oprah Winfrey," *Oprah's LifeClass,* season 2, episode 27, October 19, 2011, available at http://www.oprah.com/oprahs-lifeclass/the-powerful-lesson-maya-angelou-taught-oprah-video.
6. Lisa Sharon Harper, interview with author, September 20, 2020.
7. Barack Obama, *A Promised Land* (New York: Crown, 2020).
8. Nathan P. Kalmoe and Lilliana Mason, "Lethal Mass Partisanship: Prevalence, Correlates, and Electoral Contingencies," 2019, available at https://www.dannyhayes

.org/uploads/6/9/8/5/69858539/kalmoe___mason_ncapsa
_2019_-_lethal_partisanship_-_final_lmedit.pdf.

9. Quoted in Martin Luther King Jr.'s "An Experiment of Love"
    speech, in *A Testament of Hope: The Essential Writings and
    Speeches,* ed. James M. Washington (New York: HarperCollins,
    1986), 20.

10. King, "An Experiment of Love," 19.

11. Ashley Parker, Matt Viser, and Annie Linskey, "Biden
    Struggles to Define His 'Unity' Promise for a Divided
    Nation," *Washington Post,* January 28, 2021, available at
    https://www.washingtonpost.com/politics/biden-unity/
    2021/01/28/89707242-5fe6-11eb-afbe-9a11a127d146_story
    .html.

12. "Unity," *Cambridge Dictionary,* available at https://dictionary
    .cambridge.org/us/dictionary/english/unity.

13. Parker, Viser, and Linskey, "Biden Struggles to Define His
    'Unity' Promise."

14. Austin Channing Brown, *I'm Still Here: Black Dignity in a World
    Made for Whiteness* (New York: Convergent, 2018).

15. Tina Fossella, "Human Nature, Buddha Nature: An Interview
    with John Welwood," *Tricycle,* Spring 2011, available at https://
    tricycle.org/magazine/human-nature-buddha-nature/.

16. Samara Quintero and Jamie Long, "Toxic Positivity: The Dark
    Side of Positive Vibes," Psychology Group, October 11, 2019,
    available at https://thepsychologygroup.com/toxic-positivity/.

17. Albert Einstein, as quoted in a speech delivered by Egil
    Aarvik, chairman of the Norwegian Nobel Committee, for
    the presentation of the Nobel Peace Prize for 1985, Oslo,
    December 10, 1985, available at https://www.nobelprize.org/
    prizes/peace/1985/ceremony-speech/.

18. John Lewis, *Across That Bridge: A Vision for Change and the
    Future of America* (New York: Hachette, 2012).

19. Willie James Jennings, interview with author, March 15, 2021.

2. A Nation Divided That We Cannot Stand

1. William Shakespeare, *Hamlet,* act 1, scene 4.
2. Krissah Thompson, "Kirsten Powers: A Liberal Working for Fox News," *Washington Post,* June 17, 2015, available at https://www.washingtonpost.com/lifestyle/style/kirsten -powers-an-antiabortion-antiwar-liberal-working-for-fox -news/2015/06/17/65231060-054d-11e5-a428-c984eb07 7d4e_story.html.
3. The *Washington Post* media critic Erik Wemple quoted by Graham Vyse in "The Decline of the Fox News Liberal Pundit," *New Republic,* May 24, 2017, available at https:// newrepublic.com/article/142829/decline-fox-news-liberal -pundit.
4. Kristen Powers, "What My Name Taught Me About Online Harassment," *Bustle,* September 6, 2016, available at https:// www.bustle.com/articles/180703-im-harassed-threatened -online-because-a-famous-journalist-has-a-similar-name.
5. "Trump Calls CNN 'Fake News,'" *New York Times,* January 11, 2017, available at https://www.nytimes.com/ video/us/politics/100000004865825/trump-calls-cnn-fake -news.html.
6. Jenna Johnson and Matea Gold, "Trump Calls the Media 'The Enemy of the American People,'" *Washington Post,* February 17, 2017, available at https://www.washingtonpost .com/news/post-politics/wp/2017/02/17/trump-calls-the -media-the-enemy-of-the-american-people/.
7. John Whitesides, "From Disputes to a Breakup: Wounds Still Raw After U.S. Election," Reuters, February 7, 2017, available at https://www.reuters.com/article/us-usa-trump -relationships-insight/from-disputes-to-a-breakup-wounds -still-raw-after-u-s-election-idUSKBN15M13L.
8. Madeleine Stix, Victoria Fleischer, and Samantha Guff, "They Call Themselves 'Wives of the Deplorables' Because Their Husbands Support Trump," CNN, October 29, 2020, available at https://www.cnn.com/2020/10/29/politics/ wives-of-the-deplorables-support-group/index.html.

9. Natelegé Whaley, "Dating Apps Are Getting More Political Ahead of Midterm Elections. What Does That Say about Users?" *Mic,* October 20, 2018, available at https://www.mic.com/articles/191988/dating-apps-political-midterm-2018-elections-okcupid-bumble.

10. Orlaith Farrell, "Swipe Left If You Voted for Trump," CNN, December 2017, available at https://www.cnn.com/interactive/2017/politics/state/dating-new-york-trump/.

11. Gaby Del Valle, " 'For Conservatives, by Conservatives': The Rise of Right-Wing Dating Apps," *Vox,* December 26, 2008, available at https://www.vox.com/the-goods/2018/12/26/18150322/righter-donald-daters-patrio-conservative-dating-apps.

12. Kirsten Powers, "I Was Sexually Assaulted and Thought It Was My Fault: It's Past Time for a 1980s Reckoning," *USA Today,* October 2, 2018, available at https://www.usatoday.com/story/opinion/voices/2018/10/02/christine-blasey-ford-brett-kavanaugh-sexual-assault-reckoning-column/1485754002/.

13. Allie Malloy, Kate Sullivan, and Jeff Zeleny, "Trump Mocks Christine Blasey Ford's Testimony, Tells People to 'Think of Your Son,'" CNN, October 3, 2018, available at https://www.cnn.com/2018/10/02/politics/trump-mocks-christine-blasey-ford-kavanaugh-supreme-court/index.html.

14. Lauren Frias, "Christine Blasey Ford Says She Believes It Was Her 'Duty' to Come Forward with Sexual-Assault Allegation Against Brett Kavanaugh," *Business Insider,* November 18, 2019, available at https://www.businessinsider.com/watch-christine-blasey-ford-accepts-aclu-award-for-courage-2019-11.

3. Beyond Good and Evil

1. Richard Rohr, "The Dualistic Mind," Center for Action and Contemplation, January 29, 2017, available at https://cac.org/the-dualistic-mind-2017-01-29/.

2. Richard Rohr, interview with author, October 22, 2020.
3. Joe Pierre, "What Can We Do to Combat Political Polarization?" *Psychology Today,* April 24, 2021, available at https://www.psychologytoday.com/gb/blog/psych -unseen/202104/what-can-we-do-combat-political -polarization.
4. "Political Independents: Who They Are, What They Think," Pew Research Center, March 14, 2019, available at https:// www.pewresearch.org/politics/2019/03/14/political -independents-who-they-are-what-they-think/.
5. Michael Dimock and Richard Wike, "America Is Exceptional in the Nature of Its Political Divide," Pew Research Center, Fact Tank, November 13, 2020, available at https://www .pewresearch.org/fact-tank/2020/11/13/america-is -exceptional-in-the-nature-of-its-political-divide/.
6. Eli J. Finkel et al., "Political Sectarianism in America," *Science,* October 30, 2020, available at https://pcl.stanford.edu/ research/2020/finkel science-political.pdf.
7. Alan Abramowitz and Steven Webster, "'Negative Partisanship' Explains Everything," *Politico,* September–October 2017, available at https://www.politico.com/magazine/ story/2017/09/05/negative-partisanship-explains-everything -215534/.
8. JP Sears, "How the Media Wants You to Think," AwakenWithJP, December 12, 2020, available at https:// youtu.be/b-LHdEUrGa8.
9. Augustine of Hippo, Sermon 117 (on John 1:1).
10. James Carroll, *The Truth at the Heart of the Lie: How the Catholic Church Lost Its Soul* (New York: Random House, 2021), 311.

4. The Devil You Know

1. Brian McLaren, "Recognizing Our Biases," Center for Action and Contemplation, March 1, 2021, available at https://cac .org/recognizing-our-biases-2021-03-01/.

2. Bill Bishop, *The Big Sort: Why the Clustering of Like-Minded America Is Tearing Us Apart* (New York: Mariner Books, 2009).

3. Bill Bishop, "For Most Americans, the Local Presidential Vote Was a Landslide," *Daily Yonder,* December 17, 2020, available at https://dailyyonder.com/for-most-americans-the-local-presidential-vote-was-a-landslide/2020/12/17/.

4. Daniel Yudkin, Stephen Hawkins, and Tim Dixon, "The Perception Gap: How False Impressions Are Pulling Americans Apart," More in Common, June 2019, available at https://perceptiongap.us/media/zaslaroc/perception-gap-report-1-0-3.pdf.

5. Brian Resnick, "How Politics Breaks Our Brains," *Atlantic,* September 24, 2014, available at https://www.theatlantic.com/politics/archive/2014/09/how-politics-breaks-our-brains/380600/.

6. Tara Brach, "Part 1: The Answer Is Love: Evolving Out of 'Bad Other,'" lecture, August 7, 2019, available at https://www.tarabrach.com/part-1-answer-is-love/.

7. Eli J. Finkel et al., "Political Sectarianism in America," *Science,* October 30, 2020, available at https://pcl.stanford.edu/research/2020/finkel-science-political.pdf.

8. Yudkin, Hawkins, and Dixon, "The Perception Gap."

9. Yudkin, Hopkins, and Dixon, "The Perception Gap."

10. Douglas J. Ahler and Gaurav Sood, "The Parties in Our Heads: Misperceptions About Party Composition and Their Consequences," *Journal of Politics,* April 27, 2018, available at https://www.journals.uchicago.edu/doi/10.1086/697253.

11. Kevin Vallier, interview with author, October 5, 2020.

12. Chris Bail, *Breaking the Social Media Prism: How to Make Our Platforms Less Polarizing* (Princeton: Princeton University Press, 2021).

13. Matthew Levendusky and Dominik Stecula, "Why There's Hope Joe Biden's Quest to Unify America Will Work," *USA Today,* January 21, 2021, available at https://www.usatoday.com/story/opinion/2021/01/21/why-joe-bidens-mission-unify-america-can-succeed-column/4227430001/.

14. David G. Savage, "BFFs Ruth Bader Ginsburg and Antonin Scalia Agree to Disagree," *Los Angeles Times,* June 22, 2015, available at https://www.latimes.com/local/lanow/la-na -court-odd-couple-20150622-story.html.

15. Richard Wolf, "Opera, Travel, Food, Law: The Unlikely Friendship of Ruth Bader Ginsburg and Antonin Scalia," *USA Today,* September 20, 2020, available at https://www .usatoday.com/story/news/politics/2020/09/20/supreme -friends-ruth-bader-ginsburg-and-antonin-scalia/5844533002/.

16. "Supreme Court Justices Weigh In on Antonin Scalia's Death," *USA Today,* February 14, 2016, available at https:// www.usatoday.com/story/news/politics/2016/02/14/ statements-supreme-court-death-justice-scalia/80375976.

17. Adam Liptak, "At Memorial, Scalia Remembered as Happy Combatant," *New York Times,* March 1, 2016, available at https://www.nytimes.com/2016/03/02/us/politics/ at-memorial-scalia-remembered-as-happy-combatant .html.

18. Christopher J. Scalia (@cjscalia), Twitter post, September 18, 2020, available at https://twitter.com/cjscalia/status/ 1307109093606391810.

19. Paul Kane, "Cummings and Meadows Have Almost Nothing in Common—Except a Friendship," *Washington Post,* February 28, 2019, available at https://www.washingtonpost .com/powerpost/cummings-and-meadows-have-almost -nothing-in-common—except-a-friendship/2019/02/28/ 2c9f4848-3b91 11e9-a06c-3ec8ed509d15_story.html.

20. Kevin Vallier, interview with author, October 5, 2020.

21. Jen Hatmaker (@jenhatmaker), Facebook post, January 11, 2020, available at https://www.facebook.com/permalink .php?story_fbid=2587278454704467&id=203920953040241.

22. "Ginsburg and Scalia: 'Best Buddies,'" *All Things Considered,* NPR, February 15, 2016, available at https://www.npr .org/2016/02/15/466848775/scalia-ginsburg-opera -commemorates-sparring-supreme-court-friendship.

23. "Motivated Reasoning," *Psychology Today,* available at

https://www.psychologytoday.com/gb/basics/motivated
-reasoning.

24. Levendusky and Stecula, "Why There's Hope."

25. James Druckman, interview with author, January 20, 2021.

5. When Grace Runs Out

1. Charles M. Blow, "I Know Why the Caged Bird Shrieks," *New York Times,* Campaign Stops, September 19, 2012, available at https://campaignstops.blogs.nytimes.com/2012/09/19/blow -i-know-why-the-caged-bird-shrieks/.

2. Lisa Sharon Harper, interview with author, May 16, 2020.

3. Meredith D. Clark, "Drag Them: A Brief Etymology of So-Called 'Cancel Culture,'" *Communication and the Public,* October 16, 2020, available at https://journals.sagepub.com/ doi/full/10.1177/2057047320961562.

4. Clark, "Drag Them."

5. Clark, "Drag Them."

6. Donald G. McNeil Jr., "NYTimes Peru N-Word, Part 1: Introduction," *Medium,* March 1, 2021, available at https:// donaldgmcneiljr1954.medium.com/nytimes-peru-n-word -part-one-introduction-57eb6a3e0d95.

7. Katie Robertson and Ben Smith, "Slate Suspends Podcast Host After Debate over Racial Slur," *New York Times,* February 22, 2021, available at https://www.nytimes .com/2021/02/22/business/media/slate-mike-pesca -suspended.html.

8. Robertson and Smith, "Slate Suspends Podcast Host."

9. Robertson and Smith, "Slate Suspends Podcast Host."

10. Robertson and Smith, "Slate Suspends Podcast Host."

11. Kelsey McKinney, "Slate Podcast Host Mike Pesca Suspended Following Internal Discussion About Use of Racial Slur," *Defector,* February 22, 2021, available at https://defector .com/mike-pesca-slate-suspended/.

12. McKinney, "Slate Podcast Host Mike Pesca Suspended."

13. Robertson and Smith, "Slate Suspends Podcast Host."

14. Dan Levin, "A Racial Slur, a Viral Video, and a Reckoning," *New York Times,* December 26, 2020, available at https://www .nytimes.com/2020/12/26/us/mimi-groves-jimmy-galligan -racial-slurs.html.

15. Robby Soave, "*The New York Times* Helped a Vindictive Teen Destroy a Classmate Who Uttered a Racial Slur When She Was 15," *Reason,* December 28, 2020, available at https:// reason.com/2020/12/28/new-york-times-racial-slur-teen -jimmy-galligan-mimi-groves/.

16. "Systemic Equity Assessment: A Picture of Racial Equity Challenges and Opportunities in Loudoun County Public School District," Equity Collaborative, June 6, 2019, available at https://www.lcps.org/cms/lib/VA01000195/Centricity/ domain/60/equity_initiative_documents/LCPS_Equity _Report_FINALReport12_2_19.pdf.

17. Jan Ransom, "Trump Will Not Apologize for Calling for the Death Penalty over Central Park Five," *New York Times,* June 18, 2019, available at https://www.nytimes.com/2019/ 06/18/nyregion/central-park-five-trump.html.

18. Clark Neily, "America's Criminal Justice System Is Rotten to the Core," Cato Institute, June 7, 2020, available at https:// www.cato.org/blog/americas-criminal-justice-system-rotten -core.

19. "When Martin Luther King, Jr. Addressed Social Scientists," *Psychology Today,* January 17, 2017, available at https://www .psychologytoday.com/us/blog/sound-science-sound -policy/201701/when-martin-luther-king-jr-addressed-social -scientists.

20. George Yancy, "Dear White America," *New York Times,* December 24, 2015, available at https://opinionator.blogs .nytimes.com/2015/12/24/dear-white-america/.

21. Blow, "I Know Why the Caged Bird Shrieks."

6. People Are Not Disposable

1. bell hooks, interview with Maya Angelou, *Shambhala Sun,* January 1998, available at http://www.hartford-hwp.com/archives/45a/249.html.

2. "Inmates Rush from Cells to Save Deputy's Life," *USA Today,* August 17, 2020, available at https://youtu.be/WYW1g6u9M5I.

3. Keri Janton, "Heroes Emerge Behind Bars," *Atlanta Journal-Constitution,* November 2, 2020, available at https://www.ajc.com/life/heroes-emerge-behind-bars/MGO2X4MEXZCPHO6MGURJKYTOFU/.

4. "Inmates Rush from Cells."

5. According to the ACLU, "A patchwork of state felony disfranchisement laws, varying in severity from state to state, prevent approximately 5.85 million Americans with felony (and in several states misdemeanor) convictions from voting. Confusion about and misapplication of these laws de facto disenfranchise countless other Americans." The Felony Disenfranchisement Laws (Map) is available at https://www.aclu.org/issues/voting-rights/voter-restoration/felony-disenfranchisement-laws-map.

6. Jessica Benko, "The Radical Humaneness of Norway's Halden Prison," *New York Times Magazine,* March 26, 2015, available at https://www.nytimes.com/2015/03/29/magazine/the-radical-humaneness-of-norways-halden-prison.html.

7. Miroslav Volf, *Free of Charge: Giving and Forgiving in a Culture Stripped of Grace* (Grand Rapids: Zondervan, 2006), 159.

8. Jon Ronson, *So You've Been Publicly Shamed* (New York: Riverhead, 2015), 206–209.

9. Jon Ronson, *So You've Been Publicly Shamed.*

10. Kerry Flynn, "USA Today Editor Accuses Company of Being 'Subservient to White Authority' After She Was Fired for a Tweet," CNN, March 26, 2021, available at https://www.cnn.com/2021/03/26/media/usa-today-editor-hemal-jhaveri-fired/index.html.

11. Erik Wemple, "'It's a Shot at My Reputation': Lauren Wolfe Reacts to NYT's Statement About Her Dismissal," *Washington Post,* January 25, 2021, available at https://www.washingtonpost.com/opinions/2021/01/25/lauren-wolfe-tweet-nyt-dismissal/.

12. Benjamin VanHoose, "Dixie Chicks Say Comment That 'Canceled' Them in 2003 Is 'Mild' Compared to What People Say Today," *People,* March 16, 2020, available at https://people.com/country/dixie-chicks-say-2003-cancel-comment-mild-compared-today/.

13. Jamie Lerner, "Here's Why Whoopi Goldberg Was Canceled," *Distractify,* April 5, 2021, available at https://www.distractify.com/p/why-was-whoopi-goldberg-cancelled.

14. Mike Vulpo, "Whoopi Goldberg Reflects on Losing 'Everything' After Controversial Political Remarks," E Online, September 4, 2020, available at https://www.eonline.com/news/1185320/whoopi-goldberg-reflects-on-losing-everything-after-controversial-political-remarks.

15. Yascha Mounk, "Stop Firing the Innocent," *Atlantic,* June 27, 2020, available at https://www.theatlantic.com/ideas/archive/2020/06/stop-firing-innocent/613615/.

16. Loretta Ross, interview with author, July 21, 2020.

17. Nadia Bolz-Weber, interview with author, July 21, 2020.

18. Loretta Ross, interview with author, July 21, 2020.

19. Helen Lewis, "How Capitalism Drives Cancel Culture," *Atlantic,* July 14, 2020, available at https://www.theatlantic.com/international/archive/2020/07/cancel-culture-and-problem-woke-capitalism/614086/.

20. Rebecca Mead, "The Troll Slayer: A Cambridge Classicist Takes on Her Sexist Detractors," *New Yorker,* August 25, 2014, available at https://www.newyorker.com/magazine/2014/09/01/troll-slayer.

21. Richard Rohr, "The Scapegoat Mechanism," Center for Action and Contemplation, April 30, 2017, available at https://cac.org/the-scapegoat-mechanism-2017-04-30/.

22. UK Parliament, "Witchcraft," available at https://www

.parliament.uk/about/living-heritage/transformingsociety/
private-lives/religion/overview/witchcraft/.

23. Sarah Maslin Nir, "White Woman Is Fired After Calling Police on Black Man in Central Park," *New York Times,* May 26, 2020, available at https://www.nytimes.com/2020/05/26/nyregion/amy-cooper-dog-central-park.html.

24. Eric M. Johnson, "Boeing Communications Chief Resigns over Decades-Old Article on Women in Combat," Reuters, July 2, 2020, available at https://www.reuters.com/article/us-boeing-resignation/boeing-communications-chief-resigns-over-decades-old-article-on-women-in-combat-idUSKBN24334J.

25. Katie Robertson, "Teen Vogue Editor Resigns After Fury Over Racist Tweets," *New York Times,* March 18, 2021, available at https://www.nytimes.com/2021/03/18/business/media/teen-vogue-editor-alexi-mccammond.html.

7. Through a Glass Darkly

1. Anaïs Nin as quoted in Deb Amlen, "We Do Not See Things as They Are," *New York Times,* August 4, 2017, available at https://www.nytimes.com/2017/08/04/crosswords/daily-puzzle-2017-08-05.html.

2. Brené Brown, *Rising Strong: How the Ability to Reset Transforms the Way We Live, Love, Parent, and Lead* (New York: Spiegel & Grau, 2015), 110.

3. Courtney Leak, interview with author, April 14, 2021.

4. Christine Runyan, "What's Happening in Our Nervous Systems?" *On Being with Krista Tippett* (podcast), March 18, 2021, available at https://onbeing.org/programs/christine-runyan-whats-happening-in-our-nervous-systems/#transcript.

5. Resmaa Menakem, *My Grandmother's Hands: Racialized Trauma and the Pathway to Mending Our Hearts and Bodies* (Las Vegas: Central Recovery Press, 2017).

6. Courtney Leak, interview with author, April 14, 2021.

7. Runyan, "What's Happening?"

8. Courtney Leak, interview with author, April 14, 2021.
9. Lillian Comas-Diaz, Gordon Nagayama Hall, and Helen A. Neville, "Racial Trauma: Theory, Research, and Healing," American Psychological Association, PsycNET, available at https://psycnet.apa.org/fulltext/2019-01033-001.html.
10. Allison Klein, "A Sexist Troll Attacked Sarah Silverman; She Responded by Helping Him with His Problems," *Washington Post,* January 8, 2018, available at https://www .washingtonpost.com/news/inspired-life/wp/2018/01/08/a -man-trolled-sarah-silverman-on-twitter-she-ended-up -helping-him-with-his-medical-problems/.
11. "Take the ACE Quiz—And Learn What It Does and Doesn't Mean," Center on the Developing Child, available at https:// developingchild.harvard.edu/media-coverage/take-the-ace -quiz-and-learn-what-it-does-and-doesnt-mean/.
12. "About the CDC-Kaiser ACE Study," Centers for Disease Control and Prevention, available at https://www.cdc.gov/ violenceprevention/aces/about.html?CDC_AA_refVal=https %3A%2F%2Fwww.cdc.gov%2Fviolenceprevention%2 Facestudy%2Fabout.html.
13. "Preventing Adverse Childhood Experiences," Centers for Disease Control and Prevention, available at https://www.cdc .gov/violenceprevention/aces/fastfact.html.
14. Courtney Leak, interview with author, April 14, 2021.
15. Austin Houghtaling, interview with author, April 28, 2021.

8. What Goes in Must Come Out

1. Jessica Bennett, "What If Instead of Calling People Out, We Called Them In?" *New York Times,* November 19, 2020, available at https://www.nytimes.com/2020/11/19/style/ loretta-ross-smith-college-cancel-culture.html.
2. Hilary Andersson, "Social Media Apps Are 'Deliberately' Addictive to Users," BBC, July 4, 2018, available at https:// www.bbc.com/news/technology-44640959.
3. Yazin Akkawi, "7 Somewhat Easy Ways to Curb Your

Smartphone Addiction," *Medium,* June 25, 2018, available at https://medium.com/swlh/7-ways-to-curb-your-smartphone -addiction-and-increase-productivity-d295fe892fc.

4. Adam Hughes, "A Small Group of Prolific Users Account for a Majority of Political Tweets Sent by U.S. Adults," Pew Research Center, October 23, 2019, available at https://www .pewresearch.org/fact-tank/2019/10/23/a-small-group-of -prolific-users-account-for-a-majority-of-political-tweets-sent -by-u-s-adults/.

5. Kirsten Powers (@kirstenpowers), Twitter post, February 18, 2019, available at https://twitter.com/kirstenpowers/ status/1097550883443875841.

6. Austin Houghtaling, interview with author, April 28, 2021.

7. Tarek Abdelzaher et al., "The Paradox of Information Access: Growing Isolation in the Age of Sharing," April 4, 2020, published in Cornell University's arXiv, available at https://deepai.org/publication/the-paradox-of-information -access-growing-isolation-in-the-age-of-sharing.

8. Daniel Yudkin, Stephen Hawkins, and Tim Dixon, "The Perception Gap," More in Common, June 2019, available at https://perceptiongap.us/media/zaslaroc/perception-gap -report-1-0-3.pdf.

9. James N. Druckman, interview with author, January 20, 2021.

10. Arthur C. Brooks, "Our Culture of Contempt," *New York Times,* March 2, 2019, available at https://www.nytimes .com/2019/03/02/opinion/sunday/political-polarization .html.

11. Amanda Ripley, *High Conflict: Why We Get Trapped and How We Get Out* (New York: Simon & Schuster, 2021).

12. Gallup and Knight Foundation, "American Views 2020: Trust, Media and Democracy," August 4, 2020, available at https:// knightfoundation.org/reports/american-views-2020-trust -media-and-democracy/.

13. Jonah Goldberg, "Releash the Kraken," *Dispatch,* December 11, 2020, available at https://gfile.thedispatch .com/p/release-the-kraken.

14. Yudkin, Hawkins, and Dixon, "The Perception Gap."

15. Courtney Leak, interview with author, April 14, 2021.

16. Stuart Soroka, Patrick Fournier, and Lilach Nir, "Cross-National Evidence of a Negativity Bias in Psychophysiological Reactions to News," *Proceedings of the National Academy of Sciences,* September 17, 2019, available at https://www.pnas .org/content/116/38/18888.

9. Just Say No

1. Henry Cloud and John Townsend, *Boundaries: When to Say Yes, How to Say No to Take Control of Your Life* (Grand Rapids: Zondervan, 1992).

2. John Draper, interview with author, May 1, 2021.

3. Ruby Sales, interview with author, July 23, 2020.

4. Courtney Leak, interview with author, April 14, 2021.

5. Daniel A. Cox, Jacqueline Clemence, and Eleanor O'Neil, "Partisan Attachment: How Politics Is Changing Dating and Relationships in the Trump Era," American Enterprise Institute, February 6, 2020, available at https://www.aei.org/ research-products/report/partisan-attachment-how-politics -is-changing-dating-and-relationships-in-the-trump-era/.

6. Matthew 7:6 NIV.

10. Clothe Yourselves with Humility

1. Thomas Merton, *No Man Is an Island* (Boston: Shambhala, 2005).

2. Kris Straub, "On Research," *Chainsawsuit,* September 16, 2014, available at https://libraryguides.cobleskill.edu/sources.

3. Jacqui Lewis, "Why Can't We See?" *Learning How to See with Brian McLaren* (podcast), October 2, 2020, available at https:// cac.org/podcasts/why-cant-we-see/.

4. Adam Grant, *Think Again: The Power of Knowing What You Don't Know* (New York: Viking, 2021).

5. Jonathan Haidt, *The Righteous Mind: Why Good People Are Divided by Politics and Religion* (New York: Pantheon Books, 2012), 55.

6. Adam Grant, *Think Again.*

7. Brian Resnick, "Intellectual Humility: The Importance of Knowing You Might Be Wrong," *Vox,* January 4, 2019, available at https://www.vox.com/science-and-health/2019/1/4/17989224/intellectual-humility-explained-psychology-replication.

8. Adam Nagourney, "Clinton Says Party Failed Midterm Test over Security Issue," *New York Times,* December 4, 2002, available at https://www.nytimes.com/2002/12/04/us/clinton-says-party-failed-midterm-test-over-security-issue.html.

9. Proverbs 16:18 KJV.

10. 1 Peter 5:5 ESV.

11. Colossians 3:12 NIV.

12. Haidt, *The Righteous Mind.*

13. Jay J. Van Bavel and Andrea Pereira, "The Partisan Brain: An Identity-Based Model of Political Belief," *Trends in Cognitive Sciences,* February 20, 2018, available at https://doi.org/10.1016/j.tics.2018.01.004.

14. Debbie Elliot and Laurel Wamsley, "Alabama Governor Signs Abortion Ban Into Law," *Morning Edition,* NPR, May 14, 2019 available at http://www.npr.org/2019/05/14/723312937/alabama-lawmakers-passes-abortion-ban.

15. Rick Santorum, *Anderson Cooper 360°,* season 16, episode 174, CNN, May 14, 2019, transcript, available at http://transcripts.cnn.com/TRANSCRIPTS/1905/15/acd.01.html.

16. Lindsay Schnell, "Jews, Outraged by Restrictive Abortion Laws, Are Invoking the Hebrew Bible in the Debate," *USA Today,* July 24, 2019, available at https://www.usatoday.com/story/news/nation/2019/07/24/abortion-laws-jewish-faith-teaches-life-does-not-start-conception/1808776001/.

17. David Van Biema, "One Psalm, Two Causes, Two Meanings," *Washington Post,* March 28, 2012, available at https://www.usatoday.com/story/news/nation/2019/07/24/abortion

-laws-jewish-faith-teaches-life-does-not-start-conception/
1808776001/.

18. Psalm 139:13 NIV.

19. Santorum, *Anderson Cooper 360°.*

20. Joe Pierre, "What Can We Do to Combat Political Polarization?" *Psychology Today,* April 24, 2021, available at https://www.psychologytoday.com/gb/blog/psych -unseen/202104/what-can-we-do-combat-political -polarization.

21. David Bankenhorn, "Blue Said, Red Said," *The American Interest,* March 7, 2018, available at www.the-american-interest .com/2018/03/07/blue-said-red-said.

22. Kirsten Powers, *The Silencing: How the Left Is Killing Free Speech* (Washington, DC: Regnery, 2015).

23. Charles Spurgeon, "Christ's First and Last Subject," Sermon 329, August 19, 1860, Exeter Hall, London, England.

24. "When Martin Luther King, Jr. Addressed Social Scientists," *Psychology Today,* January 17, 2017, available at https://www .psychologytoday.com/us/blog/sound-science-sound -policy/201701/when-martin-luther-king-jr-addressed-social -scientists.

25. Samantha Sunne, "University of Alaska Fairbanks Student Newspaper Under Investigation Following Sexual Harassment Claims," Student Press Law Center, November 26, 2013, available at http://www.splc.org/article/2013/11/university -of-alaska-fairbanks-student-newspaper-under-investigation -following-sexual-harassment-cla/.

26. Denise-Marie Ordway, "UCF Instructor Placed on Leave After 'Killing Spree' Comment," *Orlando Sentinel,* April 25, 2013, available at https://www.orlandosentinel.com/news/os-xpm -2013-04-25-os-ucf-instructor-killing-spree-comment -20130425-story.html.

27. Phillip Nieto, "An Interview with Ben Shapiro: Social Justice, Free Speech, and Transgender Pronouns," *The Los Angeles Loyolan,* April 9, 2019, available at http://www.laloyolan.com/ opinion/an-interview-with-ben-shapiro-social-justice-free

-speech-and-transgender-pronouns/article_229644e1-0052
-58c0-a441-e47724c05c93.html.

28. Isabel Knight, "Students Share Mixed Responses to George/
West Collection," *The Phoenix,* February 13, 2014, available
at https://swarthmorephoenix.com/2014/02/13/students
-share-mixed-responses-to-georgewest-collection/.

29. Jonathan Haidt (@JonHaidt), Twitter post, May 6, 2019,
available at https://twitter.com/jonhaidt/
status/1125355606087544832.

30. Shunryu Suzuki, *Zen Mind, Beginner's Mind: Informal Talks on Zen
Meditation and Practice* (Boston: Shambhala, 2006).

31. Michael Casey, *The Road to Eternal Life: Reflections on the Prologue
of Benedict's Rule* (Collegeville, MN: Liturgical Press, 2012).

32. Pope Francis, *Let Us Dream: The Path to a Better Future* (New
York: Simon & Schuster, 2020).

33. Matthew 7:5 NIV.

11. Pathways to Repair

1. Desmond Tutu, "Statement by Archbishop Desmond Tutu
on His Appointment to the Truth and Reconciliation
Commission," November 30, 1995, available at https://www
.justice.gov.za/trc/media/trc-media-pr-1995-2000.pdf.

2. Ben M. Tappin and Ryan T. McKay, "The Illusion of Moral
Superiority," *Social Psychological and Personality Science,*
October 19, 2016, available at https://journals.sagepub.com/
doi/pdf/10.1177/1948550616673878.

3. Tappin and McKay, "The Illusion of Moral Superiority."

4. Tappin and McKay, "The Illusion of Moral Superiority."

5. Tappin and McKay, "The Illusion of Moral Superiority."

6. "Bonus: Rabbi Danya Ruttenberg," *The Confessional with Nadia
Bolz-Weber* (podcast), July 22, 2020, available at https://
nadiabolzweber.com/rabbi-danya-ruttenberg/.

7. Rabbi Danya Ruttenberg, interview with author, February 9,
2021.

8. "Bonus: Rabbi Danya Ruttenberg."

9. Ruttenberg, *The Confessional.*

10. George Yancy, "Dear White America," *New York Times,* December 24, 2015, available at https://opinionator.blogs .nytimes.com/2015/12/24/dear-white-america/.

11. Resolution on Racial Reconciliation on the 150th Anniversary of the Southern Baptist Convention, Annual Meeting, June 1, 1995, available at https://www.sbc.net/resource-library/ resolutions/resolution-on-racial-reconciliation-on-the-150th -anniversary-of-the-southern-baptist-convention/.

12. Interview with David W. Key (Director of Baptist Studies at Emory's Candler School of Theology for nearly two decades), March 27, 2021.

13. Sandra Gonzalez, "Justin Timberlake Apologizes to Britney Spears and Janet Jackson," CNN, February 12, 2021, available at https://www.cnn.com/2021/02/12/entertainment/justin -timberlake-apology-britney-spears-janet-jackson/index.html.

14. Margot Finn, "I Had a Late Term Abortion, President Trump and Pro-Lifers Have No Right to Call Me a Murderer," *Slate,* February 7, 2019, available at https://slate.com/ technology/2019/02/late-term-abortion-support-group -lessons-trust-myself-women.html.

15. Kate Carson, "I Had a Later Abortion Because I Couldn't Give My Baby Girl Both Life and Peace," *USA Today,* February 19, 2019, available at https://www.usatoday.com/ story/opinion/voices/2019/02/19/late-term-abortion -donald-trump-ben-sasse-state-union-column/2881880002/.

16. Kirsten Powers, "'Heartbeat Bills' Reveal Extremist Anti-Abortion View That Values Unborn over Women," *USA Today,* May 14, 2019, available at https://www.usatoday.com/ story/opinion/2019/05/14/heartbeat-bills-anti-abortion -laws-late-term-women-christian-column/1190340001/.

17. Sarah Mimms, "Republicans Are Calling for 'Unity' After They Voted to Try to Overturn the Election Following the Deadly Capitol Attack," *Buzzfeed News,* January 9, 2021, available at https://www.buzzfeednews.com/article/ sarahmimms/republicans-object-biden-win-unity-capitol -attack.

12. Embrace Healthy Conflict

1. Alanna Vagianos, "Ruth Bader Ginsburg Tells Young Women: 'Fight for the Things You Care About,'" *Huffington Post*, June 2, 2015, available at https://www.huffpost.com/entry/ruth-bader-ginsburg-fight-for-the-things-you-care-about_n_7492630.

2. Barbara Brown Taylor, *Always a Guest: Speaking of Faith Far from Home* (Louisville: Westminster John Knox, 2020), 38.

3. Matthew 5:9.

4. Tihomir Kukolja, interview with author, November 18, 2020.

5. Jemar Tisby, interview with author, August 6, 2020.

6. Tisby, interview with author.

7. Jason Marsh, "How to Turn a Toxic Conflict into a Good One," Greater Good Science Center, April 30, 2021, available at https://greatergood.berkeley.edu/article/item/how_to_turn_a_toxic_conflict_into_a_good_one.

8. Marsh, "How to Turn a Toxic Conflict into a Good One."

9. "LGBT Rights," Gallup Poll, May 2021, available at https://news.gallup.com/poll/1651/gay-lesbian-rights.aspx.

10. Joshua Kalla and David Broockman, "Reducing Exclusionary Attitudes Through Interpersonal Conversation: Evidence from Three Field Experiments," *American Political Science Review*, February 3, 2020, available at https://www.cambridge.org/core/journals/american-political-science-review/article/abs/reducing-exclusionary-attitudes-through-interpersonal-conversation-evidence-from-three-field-experiments/4AA5B97806A4CAFBAB0651F5DAD8F223#.

11. Mike Cummings, "Study Finds Non-Judgmental, Personal Approach Can Reduce Prejudice," *Yale News*, February 7, 2020, available at https://news.yale.edu/2020/02/07/study-finds-non-judgmental-personal-approach-can-reduce-prejudice.

12. Emily Kubin, Curtis Puryear, Chelsea Schein, and Kurt Gray, "Personal Experiences Bridge Moral and Political Divides Better Than Facts," *Proceedings of the National Academy of*

Sciences, February 9, 2021, available at https://www.pnas.org/content/pnas/118/6/e2008389118.

13. Kurt Gray, "Why Sharing Personal Stories Is More Important Than Facts in Bridging Political Divide," *USA Today,* January 27, 2021, available at https://www.usatoday.com/story/opinion/2021/01/27/how-reduce-political-polarization-share-personal-stories-column/4257379001/.

14. Brian Resnick, "These Scientists Can Prove It's Possible to Reduce Prejudice," *Vox,* April 8, 2016, available at https://www.vox.com/2016/4/7/11380974/reduce-prejudice-science-transgender.

15. Brian Resnick, "How to Talk Someone out of Bigotry," *Vox,* January 29, 2020, available at https://www.vox.com/2020/1/29/21065620/broockman-kalla-deep-canvassing.

16. Resnick, "How to Talk Someone out of Bigotry."

17. Kubin, Puryear, Schein, and Gray, "Personal Experiences Bridge Moral and Political Divides Better Than Facts."

18. Brian McLaren, *Why Don't They Get It? Overcoming Bias in Others (and Yourself)* (self-published, 2019), 63–64.

19. McLaren, *Why Don't They Get It?*

20. Paul Graham, "How to Disagree," March 2008, available at www.paulgraham.com/disagree.html.

21. Brené Brown, *Daring Greatly: How the Courage to Be Vulnerable Transforms the Way We Live, Love, Parent, and Lead* (New York: Gotham Books, 2012).

Conclusion

1. Coleman Barks, trans. *The Essential Rumi* (San Francisco: HarperOne, 1996).

2. Howard Thurman, *Jesus and the Disinherited* (Boston: Beacon Press, 1996).

ABOUT THE AUTHOR

KIRSTEN POWERS is a *New York Times* bestselling author, a *USA Today* columnist, and a senior political analyst for CNN. Her writing has been published in *The Washington Post, The Daily Beast, USA Today, The Dallas Morning News, Elle, Salon, The Wall Street Journal, The New York Observer, New York Post,* and *The American Prospect.* Raised in Fairbanks, Alaska, Powers lives in Washington, D.C., with her husband, Robert Draper, and their fur child, Lucy.

kirstenpowers.com

ABOUT THE TYPE

This book was set in Garamond, a typeface originally designed by the Parisian type cutter Claude Garamond (c. 1500–61). This version of Garamond was modeled on a 1592 specimen sheet from the Egenolff-Berner foundry, which was produced from types assumed to have been brought to Frankfurt by the punch cutter Jacques Sabon (c. 1520–80).

Claude Garamond's distinguished romans and italics first appeared in *Opera Ciceronis* in 1543–44. The Garamond types are clear, open, and elegant.